Project Management Toolbox

Ricardo Rodriguez

Contents

4

Part I: The PM Toolbox in the 21st Century

Chapter 1: The Evolving Role of the PM Toolbox

The project management toolbox is a collection of tools, techniques, and resources that project managers use to plan, execute, and monitor projects. The traditional role of the PM toolbox has been to provide project managers with the tools they need to manage projects efficiently and effectively.

However, in the 21st century, the role of the PM toolbox is evolving. Project managers are now facing a number of new challenges, such as:

- **The increasing complexity of projects**: Projects are becoming increasingly complex and interconnected, making them more difficult to manage.

- **The rapid pace of change**: The business world is changing faster than ever before, and project managers need to be able to adapt quickly to change.

- **The need for collaboration**: Project managers need to be able to collaborate effectively with stakeholders from all over the world.

To meet these challenges, project managers need a PM toolbox that is more flexible, adaptable, and collaborative than traditional PM toolboxes.

The new PM toolbox is a set of tools and resources that can be used to manage projects in a variety of different ways. It includes tools for:

- **Agile project management**: Agile project management is a flexible and iterative approach to project management that is well-suited for complex and rapidly changing projects.

- **Hybrid project management**: Hybrid project management combines elements of traditional and agile project management to create a customized approach that is tailored to the specific needs of the project.

- **Data-driven project management**: Data-driven project management uses data to make informed decisions about the project. This includes using data to identify and mitigate risks, track progress, and make predictions.

- **Collaborative project management**: Collaborative project management uses tools and techniques to facilitate collaboration between stakeholders. This includes using tools for communication, document sharing, and task management.

The new PM toolbox is also more adaptable than traditional PM toolboxes. It can be customized to fit the specific needs of each project and can be scaled up or down as needed.

The evolving role of the PM toolbox is having a significant impact on project management. Project managers are now able to use a wider range of tools and techniques to manage projects more effectively. This is leading to better outcomes for projects and organizations.

Here are some specific examples of how the PM toolbox is evolving in the 21st century:

- **The use of artificial intelligence (AI) and machine learning (ML) to automate tasks and make predictions.** AI and ML can be used to automate tasks such as risk identification, scheduling, and progress tracking. They can also be used to make predictions about the project, such as the likelihood of delays or cost overruns.

- **The use of cloud-based PM tools.** Cloud-based PM tools are accessible from anywhere with an internet connection, making them ideal for collaborative projects with team members located around the world. Cloud-based PM tools also tend to be more scalable and affordable than traditional on-premise PM tools.

- **The use of mobile PM apps.** Mobile PM apps allow project managers to stay on top of their projects from anywhere. Mobile PM apps can be used to track progress, communicate with stakeholders, and manage tasks.

Chapter 2: Project Management in a Digital World

Project management in a digital world is the process of using digital tools and technologies to plan, execute, and monitor projects. Digital project management tools and technologies can help project managers to:

- Improve communication and collaboration: Digital project management tools can help project managers to communicate and collaborate more effectively with team members and stakeholders. For example, project managers can use video conferencing tools to hold virtual meetings, and they can use document sharing tools to share documents and collaborate on projects.

- Increase efficiency and productivity: Digital project management tools can help project managers to increase efficiency and productivity by automating tasks and streamlining processes. For example, project managers can use time tracking tools to track the time that team members spend on tasks, and they can use project management software to track the progress of the project and identify potential problems early on.

- Make better decisions: Digital project management tools can help project managers to make better decisions by providing them with real-time data and insights. For example, project managers can use data analytics tools to identify trends and patterns in the project data, and they can use machine learning tools to predict the future performance of the project.

Here are some specific examples of how digital project management tools and technologies can be used to manage projects:

- **Work breakdown structure (WBS) tools**: WBS tools can be used to create and manage the WBS, which is a hierarchical decomposition of the project into smaller, more manageable tasks.

- **Gantt chart tools**: Gantt chart tools can be used to create and manage Gantt charts, which are visual representations of the project schedule.

- **Earned value management (EVM) tools**: EVM tools can be used to track the progress of the project and identify potential problems early on.

- **Risk management tools**: Risk management tools can be used to identify, assess, and mitigate risks to the project.

- **Communication management tools**: Communication management tools can be used to facilitate communication and collaboration between team members and stakeholders.

- **Document sharing tools**: Document sharing tools can be used to share documents and collaborate on projects.

Project management in a digital world is essential for success in today's business environment. By using digital tools and technologies, project managers can improve communication and collaboration, increase efficiency and productivity, and make better decisions.

Here are some additional tips for project management in a digital world:

- **Choose the right tools for your project**: There are a wide variety of digital project management tools and technologies available. It is important to choose the tools that are right for your project's specific needs and budget.

- **Use tools to support your project management processes**: Digital project management tools can be used to support all of the key project management processes, such as planning, executing, monitoring, and closing.

- **Train your team on how to use the tools**: It is important to train your team on how to use the digital project management tools that you have chosen. This will help to ensure that the tools are used effectively and that the project is successful.

- **Monitor the use of the tools**: It is important to monitor the use of the digital project management tools to ensure that they are being used effectively. This may involve tracking the time that team members spend using the tools and collecting feedback from team members on the tools.

Chapter 3: Building a PM Toolbox for Agile and Hybrid Projects

Building a PM toolbox for agile and hybrid projects requires a different approach than building a PM toolbox for traditional projects. Agile and hybrid projects are more complex and uncertain, and they require a more flexible and adaptable approach to project management.

Here are some tips for building a PM toolbox for agile and hybrid projects:

- **Start with the basics**: Your PM toolbox should include the basic project management tools and techniques, such as work breakdown structure (WBS), Gantt chart, and earned value management (EVM). These tools and techniques can be used to manage both agile and hybrid projects.

- **Add tools and techniques for agile and hybrid project management**: Once you have the basic project management tools and techniques in place, you can start to add tools and techniques that are specific to agile and hybrid project management. For example, you may want to add tools for agile estimation, backlog management, and sprint planning.

- **Choose tools that are compatible with each other**: It is important to choose tools that are compatible with each other. This will make it easier to integrate the tools and to share data between them.

- **Tailor the PM toolbox to your specific needs**: Every project is different, so it is important to tailor the PM toolbox to the specific needs of your project. For example, you may want to add tools and techniques that are specific to your industry or domain.

Here are some specific examples of tools and techniques that you may want to include in your PM toolbox for agile and hybrid projects:

- **Agile estimation tools**: Agile estimation tools can be used to estimate the effort required to complete tasks and user stories.

- **Backlog management tools**: Backlog management tools can be used to manage the product backlog and the sprint backlog.

- **Sprint planning tools**: Sprint planning tools can be used to plan and manage sprints.

- **Kanban boards**: Kanban boards can be used to visualize the workflow and to track the progress of tasks.

- **Collaboration tools**: Collaboration tools can be used to facilitate communication and collaboration between team members and stakeholders.

- **Data analytics tools**: Data analytics tools can be used to identify trends and patterns in the project data, and to predict the future performance of the project.

It is important to note that there is no one-size-fits-all PM toolbox for agile and hybrid projects. The best PM toolbox for your project will depend on the specific needs of your project and your team.

Here are some additional tips for building and using a PM toolbox for agile and hybrid projects:

- **Get buy-in from your team**: It is important to get buy-in from your team on the PM toolbox that you are building. This will help to ensure that the team is comfortable using the tools and that they are used effectively.

- **Provide training**: Provide training to your team on how to use the PM toolbox. This will help to ensure that the tools are used effectively and that the team is able to maximize the benefits of the tools.

- **Monitor the use of the tools**: Monitor the use of the PM toolbox to ensure that it is being used effectively. This may involve tracking the time that team members spend using the tools and collecting feedback from team members on the tools.

- **Make changes as needed**: The PM toolbox is a living document, so be sure to make changes as needed. This may involve adding new tools, removing tools, or updating the way that the tools are used.

Chapter 4: Measuring the Value of the PM Toolbox

Measuring the value of the PM toolbox can be challenging, but it is important to do so in order to justify the investment in tools and resources. There are a number of different ways to measure the value of the PM toolbox, including:

- **Project success rates**: Track the percentage of projects that are completed on time, on budget, and to the required quality standards.

- **Project cost savings**: Estimate the cost savings that are achieved by using the PM toolbox to manage projects more efficiently and effectively.

- **Customer satisfaction**: Survey customers to assess their satisfaction with the projects that are delivered using the PM toolbox.

- **Team productivity**: Track the team's productivity and identify any improvements that can be attributed to the use of the PM toolbox.

- **Risk reduction**: Identify and assess the risks that are mitigated by using the PM toolbox.

Here are some specific examples of how to measure the value of the PM toolbox:

- **Use a project management dashboard to track key project metrics, such as schedule, budget, and quality.** This will help you to identify any potential problems early on and to take corrective action.

- **Compare the performance of projects that are managed using the PM toolbox to the performance of projects that are managed without the PM toolbox.** This will help you to identify the benefits of using the PM toolbox.

- **Survey customers to assess their satisfaction with the projects that are delivered using the PM toolbox.** This will help you to identify any areas where the PM toolbox can be improved.

- **Track the team's productivity and identify any improvements that can be attributed to the use of the PM toolbox.** This will help you to justify the investment in the PM toolbox.

- **Identify and assess the risks that are mitigated by using the PM toolbox.** This will help you to quantify the value of the PM toolbox in terms of risk reduction.

It is important to note that there is no single metric that can be used to measure the value of the PM toolbox. The best approach is to use a combination of metrics to get a comprehensive understanding of the value of the PM toolbox.

Here are some additional tips for measuring the value of the PM toolbox:

- **Set clear goals and objectives:** Before you start measuring the value of the PM toolbox, it is important to set clear goals and objectives. What do you want to achieve by using the PM toolbox? Once you know what you want to achieve, you can develop metrics to track your progress.

- **Use a variety of metrics**: No single metric can tell you the whole story. Use a variety of metrics to get a comprehensive understanding of the value of the PM toolbox.

- **Track your progress over time**: It is important to track your progress over time in order to identify trends and patterns. This will help you to identify what is working and what is not working.

- **Share your results with others**: Share your results with others, such as your team, your stakeholders, and your management. This will help to raise awareness of the value of the PM toolbox and to get buy-in for using the PM toolbox to manage projects.

Part II: Essential PM Tools and Techniques

Chapter 5: Project Selection and Portfolio Management

Project selection and portfolio management (PPM) are essential tools and techniques for project managers. PPM helps project managers to select the right projects to invest in and to manage the portfolio of projects in a way that maximizes the value of the portfolio for the organization.

Project selection is the process of identifying and evaluating potential projects to determine which ones to invest in. Project selection is a critical process because it can have a significant impact on the organization's success.

There are a number of different project selection methods, including:

- **Scoring models**: Scoring models assign weights to different project criteria, such as financial return, strategic alignment, and risk. Projects are then scored based on these criteria, and the projects with the highest scores are selected.

- **Cost-benefit analysis**: Cost-benefit analysis compares the estimated costs and benefits of a project to determine whether the project is a good investment.

- **Payback period**: The payback period is the amount of time it takes to recover the initial investment in a project. Projects with shorter payback periods are typically considered to be more attractive investments.

- **Net present value (NPV)**: NPV is a financial metric that calculates the present value of all future cash flows associated with a project. Projects with positive NPVs are typically considered to be good investments.

Portfolio management is the process of managing the portfolio of projects in a way that maximizes the value of the portfolio for the organization. Portfolio management involves balancing the different risks and rewards associated with the different projects in the portfolio.

There are a number of different portfolio management tools and techniques, including:

- **Portfolio matrix**: A portfolio matrix is a tool that can be used to visualize the different projects in the portfolio and their associated risks and rewards.

- **Project prioritization**: Project prioritization involves ranking the projects in the portfolio based on their importance to the organization.

- **Resource allocation**: Resource allocation involves assigning resources to the different projects in the portfolio.

- **Risk management**: Risk management involves identifying, assessing, and mitigating the risks associated with the projects in the portfolio.

PPM is an essential tool for project managers who want to select the right projects to invest in and to manage the portfolio of projects in a way that maximizes the value of the portfolio for the organization.

Here are some additional tips for project selection and portfolio management:

- **Align projects with the organization's strategic goals**: Projects should be aligned with the organization's strategic goals in order to ensure that the organization is investing in the right projects.

- **Consider all stakeholders**: When selecting projects and managing the portfolio, it is important to consider all stakeholders, including customers, employees, and shareholders.

- **Be flexible and adaptable**: The business environment is constantly changing, so it is important to be flexible and adaptable when selecting projects and managing the portfolio.

- **Monitor the portfolio regularly**: The portfolio should be monitored regularly to ensure that it is still aligned with the organization's strategic goals and that the projects in the portfolio are still on track.

Compare Project Selection and Portfolio Management

Project selection is the process of choosing which projects to undertake, given the organization's limited resources and strategic goals. It is a critical step in ensuring that the organization's investments are used wisely and that the most important projects are prioritized.

Portfolio management is the process of managing a collection of projects, programs, and other activities in a way that maximizes the organization's overall value. It involves selecting, prioritizing, and managing projects to achieve the organization's strategic goals and objectives.

Comparison and contrast:

Characteristic	Project selection	Portfolio management
Focus	Selecting individual projects	Managing a collection of projects
Timeframe	Short-term (typically 1-3 years)	Long-term (typically 3-5 years or more)
Goals	To select the projects that will deliver the greatest value to the organization	To maximize the value of the organization's portfolio of projects
Inputs	Organizational strategy, project proposals, resource constraints	Organizational strategy, project proposals, resource constraints, portfolio performance
Outputs	A list of selected projects	A prioritized list of projects, a portfolio plan, and regular portfolio performance updates

Key differences:

- Project selection is a one-time event, while portfolio management is an ongoing process.

- Project selection focuses on individual projects, while portfolio management focuses on the collection of projects as a whole.

- Project selection is typically done on a shorter timeframe than portfolio management.
- Project selection inputs are typically limited to organizational strategy, project proposals, and resource constraints. Portfolio management inputs also include portfolio performance.
- Project selection outputs are typically a list of selected projects. Portfolio management outputs are typically a prioritized list of projects, a portfolio plan, and regular portfolio performance updates.

Example:

A company is considering three new projects:

- A new product launch that is expected to generate $10 million in revenue in the first year.
- A process improvement project that is expected to save the company $5 million in annual costs.
- A customer relationship management (CRM) system that is expected to increase sales by 10%.

The company has a limited budget and cannot undertake all three projects at the same time. To select the best project, the company would need to consider its strategic goals, the project proposals, and its resource constraints.

Once the company has selected the best project, it would need to manage it effectively to ensure that it is completed on time and on budget, and that it delivers the expected benefits. The company would also need to monitor the performance of the project and make adjustments as needed.

Project selection tools and techniques are used to identify, evaluate, and prioritize projects. Some common tools and techniques include:

- **Checklists**: Checklists are a simple way to evaluate projects against a set of criteria, such as alignment with strategic goals, feasibility, and risk.

- **Scoring models**: Scoring models assign points to projects based on a set of criteria. The projects with the highest scores are typically selected.

- **Analytical hierarchy process (AHP)**: AHP is a more complex scoring model that allows decision-makers to weigh the importance of different criteria.

- **Financial models**: Financial models, such as net present value (NPV) and internal rate of return (IRR), can be used to evaluate the financial feasibility of projects.

Portfolio management tools and techniques are used to manage a collection of projects and programs in a way that maximizes the organization's overall value. Some common tools and techniques include:

- **Portfolio management software**: Portfolio management software can be used to track the progress of projects, manage resources, and identify potential risks.

- **Portfolio dashboards**: Portfolio dashboards provide a visual overview of the portfolio's performance.

- **Portfolio roadmaps**: Portfolio roadmaps show how projects are interconnected and how they will contribute to the organization's strategic goals.

- **Portfolio reviews**: Portfolio reviews are held regularly to assess the performance of the portfolio and make adjustments as needed.

Here are some guidelines for selecting and using project selection and portfolio management tools and techniques:

- **Align tools and techniques with organizational goals and objectives.** The tools and techniques you select should help you to achieve your organization's specific project selection and portfolio management goals and objectives.

- **Consider the size and complexity of your portfolio.** If you have a small and simple portfolio, you may not need sophisticated tools and techniques. However, if you have a large and complex portfolio, you may need to invest in more sophisticated tools and techniques.

- **Involve stakeholders in the selection process.** Get input from stakeholders, such as project managers, business unit leaders, and executives, when selecting project selection and portfolio management tools and techniques. This will help to ensure that the tools and techniques are appropriate for the needs of the organization and that they will be used effectively.

- **Provide training to users.** Once you have selected project selection and portfolio management tools and techniques, provide training to users on how to use them effectively. This will help to ensure that the tools and techniques are used to their full potential.

- **Monitor and evaluate the use of tools and techniques.** Regularly monitor and evaluate the use of project selection and portfolio management tools and techniques to ensure that they are effective and that they are meeting the needs of the organization.

Here are some additional tips for using project selection and portfolio management tools and techniques effectively:

- **Use data to drive decisions.** Project selection and portfolio management tools and techniques can help you to collect and analyze data about your projects. Use this data to drive your decisions about which projects to select, prioritize, and invest in.

- **Be flexible.** Things change, so be prepared to adjust your project selection and portfolio management tools and techniques as needed.

- **Communicate with stakeholders.** Communicate regularly with stakeholders about the project selection and portfolio management process. This will help to ensure that everyone is on the same page and that there are no surprises.

Tools and techniques:

Project selection:

- **Project selection matrix:** A tool used to evaluate projects based on a set of criteria, such as strategic alignment, financial viability, and risk profile.

- **Project scoring model:** A tool used to quantify the evaluation of projects, making it easier to compare and contrast different projects.

- **Decision tree analysis:** A tool used to identify the best course of action based on a set of possible outcomes and their associated probabilities.

Portfolio management:

- **Portfolio dashboard:** A tool used to visualize the performance of a portfolio of projects, including metrics such as cost, schedule, and risk.

- **Portfolio optimization model**: A tool used to identify the best mix of projects to achieve an organization's strategic goals and objectives.

- **Portfolio risk management**: The process of identifying, assessing, and mitigating the risks to a portfolio of projects.

Chapter 6: Project Charter and Stakeholder Analysis

The project charter and stakeholder analysis are two essential tools and techniques for project managers. The project charter is a document that formally authorizes the project and defines its scope, objectives, and deliverables. Stakeholder analysis is the process of identifying and understanding the needs, expectations, and influence of stakeholders.

Project charter

The project charter is a critical document that helps to ensure that the project is aligned with the organization's strategic goals and objectives. It also helps to set expectations for the project team and stakeholders.

The project charter should include the following information:

- Project name and description
- Project objectives
- Project scope
- Project deliverables
- Project timeline
- Project budget
- Project team members
- Project stakeholders
- Project risks and mitigation strategies
- Project approval signatures

Stakeholder analysis

Stakeholder analysis is the process of identifying and understanding the needs, expectations, and influence of stakeholders. Stakeholders are any individuals or groups who have an interest in or are affected by the project.

There are a number of different stakeholder analysis techniques, including:

- **Stakeholder identification**: The first step in stakeholder analysis is to identify all of the stakeholders. This can be done by brainstorming, reviewing project documentation, and interviewing key stakeholders.

- **Stakeholder classification**: Once the stakeholders have been identified, they should be classified based on their level of interest in and influence over the project.

- **Stakeholder prioritization**: The next step is to prioritize the stakeholders based on their level of interest in and influence over the project. This will help to ensure that the project team focuses on the most important stakeholders.

- **Stakeholder engagement planning**: The final step is to develop a stakeholder engagement plan. This plan should identify how the project team will communicate with and manage the different stakeholders.

Stakeholder analysis is an important tool for project managers because it helps to ensure that the project meets the needs of all stakeholders.

How the project charter and stakeholder analysis are essential PM tools and techniques

The project charter and stakeholder analysis are essential PM tools and techniques because they help project managers to:

- **Define the project and its scope**: The project charter helps to define the project and its scope. This is important because it helps to ensure that everyone involved in the project has a clear understanding of the project's objectives, deliverables, and timeline.

- **Identify and manage stakeholders**: Stakeholder analysis helps project managers to identify and manage stakeholders. This is important because it helps to ensure that the project meets the needs of all stakeholders and that the project team is aware of and manages any potential risks or issues.

- **Communicate with stakeholders**: The project charter and stakeholder analysis can be used to communicate with stakeholders about the project. This is important because it helps to keep stakeholders informed about the project and to get their feedback and support.

Compare Project Charter and Stakeholder Analysis Tools and Techniques

Project charter and **stakeholder analysis** are two important tools and techniques used in project management. However, they have different purposes and serve different needs.

Project charter is a formal document that outlines the purpose, scope, and authority of a project. It is typically created at the beginning of a project and serves as a reference for the project manager and team throughout the project lifecycle.

Stakeholder analysis is the process of identifying, understanding, and managing the stakeholders of a project. Stakeholders are individuals or groups who have an interest in the project or who are affected by the project's outcome.

Comparison and contrast:

Characteristic	Project charter	Stakeholder analysis
Purpose	To define the purpose, scope, and authority of a project	To identify, understand, and manage the stakeholders of a project
Timeframe	Typically created at the beginning of a project	Ongoing throughout the project lifecycle
Inputs	Project objectives, scope, constraints	Stakeholder identification, stakeholder needs and expectations
Outputs	A formal document that outlines the project charter	A list of stakeholders, their needs and expectations, and a plan for managing them
Key differences		
Primary audience	Project manager and team	Project manager and team, as well as stakeholders
Focus	The project itself	The stakeholders of the project
Level of detail	More detailed	Less detailed

Example:

A company is starting a new project to develop a new product. The project manager creates a project charter to define the purpose, scope, and authority of the project. The project charter includes the following information:

- Project name: New product development project

- Project manager: John Smith

- Project start date: 2023-08-01

- Project end date: 2024-06-30

- Project budget: $1 million

- Project objectives:
  - Develop a new product that meets the needs of the target market
  - Launch the new product on time and within budget
  - Achieve a profit of $500,000 in the first year of sales

The project manager also conducts a stakeholder analysis to identify and understand the stakeholders of the project. The stakeholder analysis identifies the following stakeholders:

- Customers
- Sales team
- Marketing team
- Engineering team
- Manufacturing team
- Executives

The project manager then develops a plan for managing the stakeholders of the project. The plan includes the following activities:

- Communicating regularly with stakeholders

- Keeping stakeholders informed of the project's progress
- Managing stakeholder expectations
- Resolving stakeholder conflicts

This is an example of how project charter and stakeholder analysis tools and techniques can be used together to ensure the successful completion of a project.

Guidelines for using project charter and stakeholder analysis tools and techniques:

- **Use the project charter to guide the project team.** The project charter should be used as a reference throughout the project lifecycle to ensure that the project stays on track and meets its objectives.

- **Involve stakeholders in the planning and execution of the project.** Stakeholders should be consulted throughout the project lifecycle to get their input and feedback. This will help to ensure that the project meets the needs of all stakeholders.

- **Communicate regularly with stakeholders.** Keep stakeholders informed of the project's progress and any changes to the project plan. This will help to manage stakeholder expectations and avoid surprises.

- **Manage stakeholder conflicts effectively.** Conflicts between stakeholders are inevitable. The project manager should have a plan in place for managing stakeholder conflicts. This plan should include steps for identifying and resolving conflicts.

Here are some specific guidelines for using project charter and stakeholder analysis tools and techniques:

Project charter

- **Be clear and concise.** The project charter should be a clear and concise document that is easy to understand for all stakeholders.

- **Be specific.** The project charter should specifically define the purpose, scope, and authority of the project.

- **Be realistic.** The project charter should be realistic in terms of the project's objectives, budget, and timeline.

- **Get stakeholder buy-in.** The project charter should be reviewed and approved by all key stakeholders before the project begins.

- **Update the project charter as needed.** The project charter should be updated throughout the project lifecycle to reflect changes in the project's scope or objectives.

Stakeholder analysis

- **Identify all stakeholders.** It is important to identify all stakeholders, both internal and external, who have an interest in the project or who are affected by the project's outcome.

- **Understand stakeholder needs and expectations.** Once the stakeholders have been identified, it is important to understand their needs and expectations. This can be done through interviews, surveys, or focus groups.

- **Classify stakeholders.** Stakeholders can be classified based on their level of interest and influence. This will help the project manager to develop a plan for managing each stakeholder group.

- **Develop a stakeholder engagement plan.** The stakeholder engagement plan should outline how the project manager will communicate and interact with stakeholders throughout the project lifecycle.

- **Manage stakeholder expectations.** It is important to manage stakeholder expectations throughout the project lifecycle. This can be done by communicating regularly with stakeholders and by keeping them informed of the project's progress.

Additional tips:

- Use data to drive decisions. Both project charter and stakeholder analysis can be data-driven processes. Use data to inform your decisions about the project's scope, objectives, and stakeholder management plan.

- Be flexible. Things change, so be prepared to adjust your project charter and stakeholder management plan as needed.

- Communicate with stakeholders. Communication is key to successful project management. Keep stakeholders informed of the project's progress and any changes to the project charter or stakeholder management plan.

Project Charter

Tools and techniques:

- **Project charter template**: A document that provides a high-level overview of the project, including its objectives, scope, constraints, and assumptions.

- **Project charter workshop**: A workshop that can be used to develop or update the project charter.

Stakeholder Analysis

Tools and techniques:

- **Stakeholder identification matrix**: A tool used to identify all of the stakeholders in a project.

- **Stakeholder power/interest matrix**: A tool used to assess the power and interest of each stakeholder in a project.

- **Stakeholder engagement plan**: A document that outlines how the project team will engage with stakeholders throughout the project lifecycle.

Chapter 7: Requirements Management and Scope Planning

Requirements management and scope planning are two essential tools and techniques for project managers. Requirements management is the process of identifying, documenting, and managing the requirements of a project. Scope planning is the process of defining the scope of a project and creating a plan to manage the scope.

Requirements management

Requirements management is a critical process for any project. Without a clear understanding of the requirements, it is impossible to deliver a product or service that meets the needs of the customer.

The requirements management process typically includes the following steps:

1. **Identify requirements:** The first step is to identify all of the requirements for the project. This can be done by brainstorming, interviewing stakeholders, and reviewing project documentation.

2. **Document requirements:** Once the requirements have been identified, they need to be documented. This can be done in a variety of ways, such as using natural language, user stories, or use cases.

3. **Analyze requirements:** Once the requirements have been documented, they need to be analyzed to ensure that they are complete, consistent, and feasible.

4. **Prioritize requirements:** Once the requirements have been analyzed, they need to be prioritized. This will help to ensure that the most important requirements are addressed first.

5. **Manage requirements changes:** Requirements are likely to change throughout the course of a project. It is important to have a process in place to manage requirements changes.

Scope planning

Scope planning is the process of defining the scope of a project and creating a plan to manage the scope. The scope of a project is the work that needs to be done to deliver the project's objectives.

The scope planning process typically includes the following steps:

1. **Define the scope:** The first step is to define the scope of the project. This includes identifying the work that needs to be done to deliver the project's objectives and excluding the work that is not necessary.

2. **Create a work breakdown structure (WBS):** A WBS is a hierarchical decomposition of the project work into smaller, more manageable tasks.

3. **Estimate the effort and cost of each task**: Once the WBS is created, the effort and cost of each task needs to be estimated.

4. **Create a schedule for the project**: Once the effort and cost of each task have been estimated, a schedule for the project can be created.

5. **Develop a scope management plan**: The scope management plan is a document that describes how the scope of the project will be managed.

How requirements management and scope planning are essential PM tools and techniques

Requirements management and scope planning are essential PM tools and techniques because they help project managers to:

- **Ensure that the project meets the needs of the customer**: Requirements management helps to ensure that the project meets the needs of the customer by identifying and managing the requirements of the project. Scope planning helps to ensure that the project meets the needs of the customer by defining the scope of the project and creating a plan to manage the scope.

- **Avoid scope creep**: Scope creep is the uncontrolled growth of the project scope. Scope planning helps to avoid scope creep by defining the scope of the project and creating a plan to manage the scope. Requirements management also helps to avoid scope creep by ensuring that the project team is aware of all the requirements of the project.

- **Deliver the project on time and on budget:** By defining the

    scope of the project and creating a plan to manage the scope,

    scope planning helps to ensure that the project is delivered on

    time and on budget. Requirements management also helps to

    ensure that the project is delivered on time and on budget by
    ensuring that the project team is aware of all the requirements

    of the project.

Compare Requirements Management and Scope Planning

Requirements management is the process of identifying, documenting, prioritizing, and managing the requirements of a project. Requirements are the needs and expectations of the stakeholders of a project.

Scope planning is the process of defining the scope of a project. The scope of a project is the work that needs to be done to complete the project.

Comparison and contrast:

Characteristic	Requirements management	Scope planning
Purpose	To identify, document, prioritize, and manage the requirements of a project	To define the scope of a project
Timeframe	Ongoing throughout the project lifecycle	Typically done at the beginning of a project
Inputs	Stakeholder needs and expectations	Project objectives, constraints, and requirements
Outputs	A requirements management plan, requirements documents, and a requirements traceability matrix	A scope statement and a work breakdown structure (WBS)
Key differences		
Primary audience	Business analysts and project managers	Project managers and project teams
Focus	The requirements of the project	The scope of the project
Level of detail	More detailed	Less detailed

Example:

A company is starting a new project to develop a new software product. The business analyst identifies the following requirements for the product:

- The product must be able to manage customer accounts and orders.

- The product must be able to generate reports on sales and inventory.

- The product must be able to integrate with the company's existing CRM system.

The business analyst then documents the requirements in a requirements document. The requirements document includes the following information:

- A description of each requirement
- The priority of each requirement
- The status of each requirement

- The traceability of each requirement to the project's objectives

The project manager then uses the requirements document to create a scope statement for the project. The scope statement defines the scope of the project in terms of the work that needs to be done to meet the requirements. The project manager also uses the requirements document to create a work breakdown structure (WBS). The WBS breaks down the work of the project into smaller and more manageable tasks.

This is an example of how requirements management and scope planning tools and techniques can be used together to ensure the successful completion of a project.

Guidelines for using requirements management and scope planning tools and techniques:

- **Use requirements management to manage the requirements of the project.** Requirements management is an ongoing process that should be used throughout the project lifecycle.

- **Use scope planning to define the scope of the project.** Scope planning is typically done at the beginning of the project, but it should be reviewed and updated as needed throughout the project lifecycle.

- **Get stakeholder buy-in.** The requirements management plan and the scope statement should be reviewed and approved by all key stakeholders before the project begins.

- **Communicate regularly with stakeholders.** Keep stakeholders informed of the project's progress and any changes to the requirements or the scope of the project.

- **Manage change effectively.** Changes to the requirements or the scope of the project are inevitable. The project manager should have a plan in place for managing change. This plan should include steps for identifying, evaluating, and approving change requests.

Here are some specific guidelines for using requirements management and scope planning tools and techniques:

Requirements management

- **Identify all requirements.** It is important to identify all requirements, both functional and non-functional. Functional requirements describe what the system should do, while non-functional requirements describe how the system should perform.

- **Document requirements in a clear and concise manner.** Requirements should be documented in a clear and concise manner that is easy to understand for all stakeholders.

- **Prioritize requirements.** Not all requirements are created equal. Some requirements are more important than others. Prioritize requirements based on their importance and the impact they will have on the business.

- **Manage requirements changes.** Requirements change over time. It is important to have a process in place for managing requirements changes. This process should include steps for identifying, evaluating, and approving change requests.

- **Use requirements traceability.** Requirements traceability is the process of tracking the relationships between requirements and other project artifacts, such as design documents, test cases, and code. Requirements traceability helps to ensure that all requirements are met and that the project is on track.

Scope planning

- **Define the scope statement.** The scope statement is a formal document that defines the scope of the project. The scope statement should include the project's objectives, deliverables, exclusions, assumptions, and constraints.

- **Create a work breakdown structure (WBS).** The WBS is a hierarchical decomposition of the work of the project. The WBS breaks down the work into smaller and more manageable tasks.
- **Estimate the time and resources required to complete each task in the WBS.** This will help to develop a realistic project schedule and budget.
- **Identify and manage risks.** Risks are events that could impact the project's schedule, budget, or quality. Identify and manage risks throughout the project lifecycle.
- **Monitor and control the project's progress.** Monitor the project's progress and compare it to the project schedule and budget. Make adjustments as needed to ensure that the project is on track.

Additional tips:

- Use data to drive decisions. Both requirements management and scope planning can be data-driven processes. Use data to inform your decisions about the requirements, the scope of the project, and the project plan.
- Be flexible. Things change, so be prepared to adjust your requirements management and scope planning processes as needed.

- Communicate with stakeholders. Communication is key to successful requirements management and scope planning. Keep stakeholders informed of the project's progress and any changes to the requirements or the scope of the project.

Tools and techniques:

Requirements management:

- **Requirements gathering techniques:** Interviews, surveys, workshops, and focus groups.

- **Requirements analysis techniques:** Use case analysis, data modeling, and business process modeling.

- **Requirements documentation techniques:** Requirements document, use case descriptions, and data flow diagrams.

- **Requirements validation techniques:** Requirements reviews, inspections, and walkthroughs.

Scope planning:

- **Scope definition techniques:** Product breakdown structure (PBS), work breakdown structure (WBS), and scope statement.

- **Scope management techniques:** Scope change management plan, scope baseline, and scope verification.

Chapter 8: Schedule Development and Cost Estimation

Schedule development and cost estimation are two essential tools and techniques for project managers. Schedule development is the process of creating a plan for how the project will be completed. Cost estimation is the process of estimating the cost of completing the project.

Schedule development

The schedule development process typically includes the following steps:

1. **Identify tasks:** The first step is to identify all of the tasks that need to be completed in order to deliver the project's objectives.

2. **Estimate the effort and cost of each task:** Once the tasks have been identified, the effort and cost of each task needs to be estimated.

3. **Sequence the tasks:** Once the effort and cost of each task have been estimated, the tasks need to be sequenced in order to minimize risk and maximize efficiency.

4. **Identify dependencies:** Dependencies are relationships between tasks that indicate that one task must be completed before another task can start.

5. **Create a schedule:** Once the tasks have been sequenced and dependencies have been identified, a schedule can be created.

Cost estimation

47

The cost estimation process typically includes the following steps:

1. **Identify cost drivers**: Cost drivers are factors that affect the cost of the project. Examples of cost drivers include labor costs, material costs, and equipment costs.

2. **Estimate the cost of each cost driver**: Once the cost drivers have been identified, the cost of each cost driver needs to be estimated.

3. **Sum the costs of the cost drivers**: To calculate the total estimated cost of the project, the costs of the individual cost drivers need to be summed.

How schedule development and cost estimation are essential PM tools and techniques

Schedule development and cost estimation are essential PM tools and techniques because they help project managers to:

- **Deliver the project on time and on budget**: By creating a plan for how the project will be completed and estimating the cost of completing the project, project managers can increase the chances of delivering the project on time and on budget.

- **Identify and manage risks**: Schedule development and cost estimation can help project managers to identify and manage risks. For example, if a project manager estimates that a task will take longer than originally planned, the project manager can take steps to mitigate the risk of the project being delayed.

- **Communicate with stakeholders**: Schedule development and cost estimation can help project managers to communicate with stakeholders about the project. For example, a project manager can use the project schedule to communicate with stakeholders about when the project is expected to be completed.

Compare Schedule Development and Cost Estimation Tools and Techniques

Schedule development is the process of creating a schedule for a project. The schedule identifies the tasks that need to be completed, the sequence in which the tasks need to be completed, and the estimated duration of each task.

Cost estimation is the process of estimating the cost of a project. The cost estimation includes the cost of materials, labor, and other resources.

Comparison and contrast:

Characteristic	Schedule development	Cost estimation
Purpose	To create a schedule for a project	To estimate the cost of a project
Timeframe	Typically done at the beginning of a project, but can be updated as needed throughout the project lifecycle	Typically done at the beginning of a project, but can be updated as needed throughout the project lifecycle
Inputs	Project objectives, scope, and constraints	Project scope, resources, and constraints
Outputs	A project schedule	A cost estimate
Key differences		
Focus	The sequence and duration of tasks	The cost of resources
Level of detail	More detailed	Less detailed

Example:

A company is starting a new project to develop a new software product. The project manager uses the project's objectives, scope, and constraints to create a project schedule. The project schedule identifies the following tasks:

- Requirements gathering and analysis

- System design
- Implementation
- Testing
- Deployment

The project manager also estimates the duration of each task.

The total duration of the project is estimated to be 6 months.

The project manager then uses the project's scope, resources, and constraints to create a cost estimate. The cost estimate includes the cost of labor, materials, and other resources. The total cost of the project is estimated to be $1 million.

This is an example of how schedule development and cost estimation tools and techniques can be used together to ensure the successful completion of a project.

Guidelines for using schedule development and cost estimation tools and techniques:

- **Use a realistic project schedule and cost estimate.** The project schedule and cost estimate should be realistic and achievable.

- **Break down the project into smaller tasks.** This will make it easier to estimate the duration and cost of each task.

- **Use historical data to estimate the duration and cost of tasks.** If possible, use historical data from similar projects to estimate the duration and cost of tasks.

- **Involve stakeholders in the schedule development and cost estimation process.** Get input from stakeholders on the project schedule and cost estimate. This will help to ensure that the schedule and cost estimate are realistic and achievable.

- **Monitor and control the project's progress and budget.** Monitor the project's progress and budget against the project schedule and cost estimate. Make adjustments as needed to ensure that the project is on track and within budget.

Schedule development tools and techniques are used to create a project schedule that defines the start and end dates of tasks, as well as the dependencies between tasks. Some common schedule development tools and techniques include:

- **Work breakdown structure (WBS):** A hierarchical decomposition of the work of the project into smaller and more manageable tasks.

- **Gantt chart:** A bar chart that shows the start and end dates of tasks, as well as the dependencies between tasks.

- **Critical path method (CPM):** A technique for identifying the critical tasks in a project and estimating the project's duration.

- **Program evaluation and review technique (PERT):** A technique for estimating the duration of a project when there is uncertainty about the duration of individual tasks.

Cost estimation tools and techniques are used to estimate the cost of a project. Some common cost estimation tools and techniques include:

- **Analogous estimating**: Estimating a project's cost based on the cost of similar projects.

- **Parametric estimating**: Estimating a project's cost based on historical data and mathematical relationships between the cost of different project components.

- **Bottom-up estimating**: Estimating a project's cost by estimating the cost of individual tasks and then summing those costs.

Chapter 9: Risk Management and Procurement Management

Risk management and procurement management are two essential PM tools and techniques.

Risk management is the process of identifying, assessing, and responding to risks that could impact the project. It is an important part of project management because it can help to reduce the likelihood and impact of negative events.

The risk management process typically includes the following steps:

1. **Identify risks:** The first step is to identify all of the risks that could impact the project. This can be done by brainstorming, interviewing stakeholders, and reviewing project documentation.

2. **Assess risks:** Once the risks have been identified, they need to be assessed to determine their likelihood and impact.

3. **Respond to risks:** Once the risks have been assessed, the project team needs to develop a plan to respond to the risks. This may involve mitigating the risks, transferring the risks, or accepting the risks.

Procurement management is the process of acquiring the goods and services that are needed to complete the project. It is an important part of project management because it can help to ensure that the project has the resources it needs to be successful.

The procurement management process typically includes the following steps:

1. **Identify needs**: The first step is to identify all of the goods and services that are needed to complete the project.

2. **Select suppliers**: Once the needs have been identified, the project team needs to select suppliers to provide the goods and services.

3. **Negotiate contracts**: Once suppliers have been selected, the project team needs to negotiate contracts with the suppliers.

4. **Manage contracts**: Once contracts have been negotiated, the project team needs to manage the contracts to ensure that the goods and services are delivered on time and on budget.

How risk management and procurement management are essential PM tools and techniques

Risk management and procurement management are essential PM tools and techniques because they help project managers to:

- **Increase the chances of success**: By identifying, assessing, and responding to risks, project managers can increase the chances of success. By acquiring the goods and services that are needed to complete the project, project managers can also increase the chances of success.

- **Reduce costs**: By mitigating risks, project managers can reduce the costs associated with those risks. By negotiating contracts with suppliers, project managers can also reduce costs.

- **Protect the organization:** By identifying and responding to risks, project managers can protect the organization from negative events. By acquiring goods and services from reputable suppliers, project managers can also protect the organization.

Compare Risk Management and Procurement

Risk management is the process of identifying, assessing, and mitigating risks to a project. **Procurement** is the process of acquiring goods and services from suppliers.

Comparison and contrast:

Characteristic	Risk management	Procurement
Purpose	To identify, assess, and mitigate risks to a project	To acquire goods and services from suppliers
Timeframe	Throughout the project lifecycle	Typically done at the beginning of a project
Inputs	Project objectives, scope, and constraints	Project requirements
Outputs	A risk management plan	A procurement plan and contracts with suppliers
Key differences		
Focus	The risks to a project	The acquisition of goods and services
Level of detail	More detailed	Less detailed

Example:

A company is starting a new project to develop a new software product. The project manager uses the project's objectives, scope, and constraints to identify potential risks. The project manager then assesses the likelihood and impact of each risk. The project manager then develops a risk management plan to mitigate the risks.

The project manager also develops a procurement plan to identify and acquire the goods and services needed for the project. The procurement plan includes the following information:

- A list of the goods and services needed
- The specifications for the goods and services
- The timeline for acquiring the goods and services

- The budget for acquiring the goods and services

The project manager then solicits bids from suppliers and awards contracts to the suppliers that meet the specifications and budget requirements.

This is an example of how risk management and procurement tools and techniques can be used together to ensure the successful completion of a project.

Guidelines for using risk management and procurement tools and techniques:

- **Involve stakeholders.** Get input from stakeholders on the risk management process and the procurement process. This will help to ensure that the risks to the project are identified and mitigated, and that the goods and services needed for the project are acquired in a timely and cost-effective manner.

- **Use data to drive decisions.** Use data to inform your decisions about the risks to the project and the procurement of goods and services.

- **Be flexible.** Things change, so be prepared to adjust the risk management and procurement processes as needed.

- **Communicate regularly.** Communicate regularly with stakeholders about the risk management process and the procurement process. This will help to ensure that everyone is on the same page and that there are no surprises.

Risk management

- **Identify risks.** The first step in risk management is to identify the risks to the project. This can be done by brainstorming, reviewing historical data, and conducting risk assessments.

- **Assess risks.** Once the risks have been identified, they need to be assessed in terms of their likelihood and impact. This can be done using a risk assessment matrix.

- **Mitigate risks.** Once the risks have been assessed, they need to be mitigated. This can be done by developing contingency plans, avoiding the risks, or transferring the risks to a third party.

- **Monitor and control risks.** Risks need to be monitored and controlled throughout the project lifecycle. This means regularly assessing the risks and making adjustments to the risk management plan as needed.

Procurement

- **Identify requirements.** The first step in procurement is to identify the goods and services needed for the project. This can be done by reviewing the project scope and developing a requirements document.

- **Develop a procurement plan.** The procurement plan should include the following information:
  - A list of the goods and services needed
  - The specifications for the goods and services
  - The timeline for acquiring the goods and services
  - The budget for acquiring the goods and services

- **Select suppliers.** The next step is to select suppliers for the goods and services needed. This can be done by soliciting bids from suppliers and evaluating the bids based on price, quality, and other factors.

- **Award contracts.** Once the suppliers have been selected, contracts need to be awarded. The contracts should clearly define the goods and services to be provided, the price, and the timeline.

- **Manage contracts.** Contracts need to be managed throughout the procurement process. This means monitoring the performance of the suppliers and making adjustments as needed.

Tools and techniques:

Risk management:

- Risk assessment matrix: A tool used to assess the likelihood and impact of risks.

- Risk register: A document that lists all of the identified risks, along with their likelihood, impact, and mitigation strategies.

- Contingency plans: Plans that are put in place to mitigate the impact of risks if they occur.

Procurement:

- Request for proposal (RFP): A document sent to potential suppliers that outlines the project requirements and solicits bids.

- Statement of work (SOW): A detailed document that describes the goods and services to be procured, as well as the terms and conditions of the contract.

- Vendor evaluation matrix: A tool used to evaluate potential suppliers based on criteria such as price, quality, and experience.

Chapter 10: Communication Management and Resource Management

Communication management and resource management are two essential PM tools and techniques.

Communication management is the process of planning, executing, monitoring, and controlling communications throughout the project life cycle. It is important for project managers to communicate effectively with stakeholders to ensure that everyone is aligned on the project goals, objectives, and deliverables.

The communication management process typically includes the following steps:

1. **Identify stakeholders**: The first step is to identify all of the stakeholders who will be impacted by the project. This may include customers, users, sponsors, team members, and other stakcholders.

2. **Analyze stakeholder needs**: Once the stakeholders have been identified, the project manager needs to analyze their needs to determine what information they need and how they want to receive it.

3. **Develop a communication plan**: The communication plan should identify the stakeholders, their needs, and how the project manager will communicate with them.

4. **Execute the communication plan**: The project manager should execute the communication plan as outlined. This may involve communicating with stakeholders through meetings, emails, status reports, and other communication channels.

5. **Monitor and control communications**: The project manager should monitor and control communications to ensure that the communication plan is effective. This may involve tracking stakeholder engagement, collecting feedback, and making changes to the communication plan as needed.

Resource management is the process of planning, acquiring, developing, managing, and disposing of resources throughout the project life cycle. It is important for project managers to manage resources effectively to ensure that the project has the people, equipment, and materials it needs to be successful.

The resource management process typically includes the following steps:

1. **Identify resource needs**: The first step is to identify all of the resources that will be needed to complete the project. This may include people, equipment, materials, and funding.

2. **Estimate resource availability**: Once the resource needs have been identified, the project manager needs to estimate the availability of the resources. This may involve identifying potential suppliers, estimating costs, and determining timelines.

3. **Acquire resources**: The project manager needs to acquire the resources that are needed to complete the project. This may involve hiring staff, purchasing equipment, and securing funding.

4. **Develop resources**: The project manager may need to develop resources, such as training staff or developing new equipment.

5. **Manage resources**: The project manager needs to manage the resources to ensure that they are used effectively and efficiently. This may involve tracking resource usage, identifying potential risks, and taking corrective action as needed.

6. **Dispose of resources**: Once the project is completed, the project manager needs to dispose of the resources in a responsible manner. This may involve returning equipment to suppliers or selling surplus materials.

How communication management and resource management are essential PM tools and techniques

Communication management and resource management are essential PM tools and techniques because they help project managers to:

- **Increase the chances of success**: By communicating effectively with stakeholders and managing resources effectively, project managers can increase the chances of success.

- **Reduce costs**: By managing resources effectively, project managers can reduce the costs associated with those resources.

- **Protect the organization**: By communicating effectively with stakeholders and managing resources effectively, project managers can protect the organization from negative events.

Compare Communication Management and Resource Management

Communication management is the process of ensuring that the right information is communicated to the right people at the right time in the right way. **Resource management** is the process of optimizing the use of resources to achieve a goal.

Characteristic	Communication management	Resource management
Purpose	To ensure that the right information is communicated to the right people at the right time in the right way	To optimize the use of resources to achieve a goal
Timeframe	Throughout the project lifecycle	Throughout the project lifecycle
Inputs	Project objectives, scope, and constraints	Project objectives, scope, constraints, and resources
Outputs	A communication plan, communication materials, and communication logs	A resource management plan, resource allocation, and resource utilization reports
Key differences		
Focus	The communication needs of the project	The resources needed for the project
Level of detail	More detailed	Less detailed

Example:

A company is starting a new project to develop a new software product. The project manager develops a communication plan to identify the communication needs of the project, the target audiences for the communication, and the communication channels to be used. The project manager also develops communication materials, such as status reports, meeting minutes, and presentations. The project manager then communicates with the stakeholders throughout the project lifecycle to keep them informed of the project's progress and to get their input.

The project manager also develops a resource management plan to identify the resources needed for the project, such as people, equipment, and materials. The project manager then allocates the resources to the tasks in the project schedule. The project manager also monitors the utilization of the resources and makes adjustments as needed.

This is an example of how communication management and resource management tools and techniques can be used together to ensure the successful completion of a project.

Guidelines for using communication management and resource management tools and techniques:

- **Involve stakeholders.** Get input from stakeholders on the communication management plan and the resource management plan. This will help to ensure that the communication and resource management needs of the project are met.

- **Use data to drive decisions.** Use data to inform your decisions about the communication and resource management needs of the project.

- **Be flexible.** Things change, so be prepared to adjust the communication management and resource management plans as needed.

- **Communicate regularly.** Communicate regularly with stakeholders about the communication management plan and the resource management plan. This will help to ensure that everyone is on the same page and that there are no surprises.

Communication management

- **Identify your stakeholders.** The first step in communication management is to identify all of the stakeholders who are interested in or affected by the project. This includes both internal and external stakeholders.

- **Understand the communication needs of your stakeholders.** Once you have identified your stakeholders, you need to understand their communication needs. What information do they need to know? How often do they need to be updated? What is their preferred communication channel?

- **Develop a communication plan.** The communication plan should identify the following:
  - The communication goals and objectives
  - The target audiences for the communication
  - The key messages to be communicated
  - The communication channels to be used
  - The communication frequency
  - The roles and responsibilities of the communication team

- **Create communication materials.** The communication materials should be clear, concise, and easy to understand. They should be tailored to the specific needs of the target audience.

- **Communicate regularly.** Communicate with your stakeholders regularly throughout the project lifecycle. Keep them informed of the project's progress, challenges, and decisions.

- **Get feedback.** Get feedback from your stakeholders on the communication. This will help you to improve your communication strategies over time.

Resource management

- **Identify the resources needed for the project.** This includes people, equipment, materials, and money.

- **Estimate the resource requirements for each task in the project schedule.** This will help you to determine the total resource requirements for the project.

- **Allocate resources to tasks.** Allocate resources to tasks in a way that maximizes efficiency and minimizes costs.

- **Monitor resource utilization.** Track the utilization of resources throughout the project lifecycle. Make adjustments as needed to ensure that resources are being used efficiently.

- **Manage resource conflicts.** Resource conflicts can occur when two or more tasks require the same resource at the same time. Identify and manage resource conflicts early on to minimize their impact on the project schedule and budget.

Communication Management

- **Tools:**

- Communication plan: A document that identifies the communication needs of the project and defines how information will be communicated to stakeholders.

- Status reports: Regular updates on the progress of the project, typically distributed to stakeholders.

- Meeting minutes: A record of the discussions and decisions made during team meetings.

- Presentation software: Software used to create and deliver presentations to stakeholders.

- Collaboration tools: Software tools that allow team members to communicate and collaborate with each other, such as Slack, Microsoft Teams, and Google Workspace.

- **Techniques:**

  - Active listening: Paying attention to the speaker, understanding their message, and responding thoughtfully.

  - Clear and concise communication: Using simple language and avoiding jargon.

  - Tailoring communication to the audience: Considering the needs and interests of the audience when communicating with them.

- o Using multiple communication channels: Using a variety of communication channels, such as email, phone, and video conferencing, to reach stakeholders.

Resource Management

- **Tools:**
    - o Resource plan: A document that identifies the resources needed for the project, such as people, equipment, and materials.
    - o Resource scheduling software: Software used to schedule resources and track their utilization.
    - o Resource budgeting software: Software used to budget for resources and track spending.
    - o Resource management dashboards: Dashboards that provide real-time insights into resource utilization and spending.

- **Techniques:**
    - o Resource forecasting: Estimating the resources needed for a project.
    - o Resource allocation: Assigning resources to tasks.

- o Resource leveling: Smoothing out the demand for resources over time.

- o Resource monitoring: Tracking the utilization of resources and making adjustments as needed.

Chapter 11: Quality Management and Team Management

Quality management and team management are two essential PM tools and techniques.

Quality management is the process of ensuring that the project meets the needs of the customer and other stakeholders. It is important for project managers to manage quality effectively to ensure that the project is successful.

The quality management process typically includes the following steps:

1. **Define quality**: The first step is to define quality. What do the customer and other stakeholders expect from the project?

2. **Plan for quality**: Once quality has been defined, the project manager needs to develop a plan to achieve quality. This may involve identifying quality standards, developing quality control procedures, and creating a quality assurance plan.

3. **Execute the quality plan**: The project manager needs to execute the quality plan as outlined. This may involve monitoring the quality of the project deliverables, taking corrective action when necessary, and reporting on quality to stakeholders.

4. **Monitor and control quality**: The project manager needs to monitor and control the quality of the project deliverables. This may involve conducting inspections, reviewing deliverables, and collecting feedback from stakeholders.

5. **Improve quality**: The project manager should continuously strive to improve the quality of the project deliverables. This may involve implementing new quality standards, procedures, and tools.

Team management is the process of planning, organizing, leading, and controlling the team to achieve the project goals. It is important for project managers to manage the team effectively to ensure that the project is successful.

The team management process typically includes the following steps:

1. **Build the team**: The first step is to build the team. This may involve identifying team members, assigning roles and responsibilities, and developing team norms.

2. **Motivate the team**: The project manager needs to motivate the team to achieve the project goals. This may involve setting clear goals and expectations, providing feedback, and recognizing and rewarding good performance.

3. **Manage conflict**: The project manager needs to manage conflict within the team. This may involve identifying the source of the conflict, mediating between team members, and developing solutions to the conflict.

4. **Develop the team**: The project manager should develop the team members by providing training and development opportunities. This will help to improve the team's skills and knowledge, and make the team more effective.

How quality management and team management are essential PM tools and techniques

Quality management and team management are essential PM tools and techniques because they help project managers to:

- **Deliver a successful project**: By managing quality and the team effectively, project managers can increase the chances of delivering a successful project.

- **Meet the needs of the customer and other stakeholders**: By managing quality and the team effectively, project managers can ensure that the project meets the needs of the customer and other stakeholders.

- **Improve the efficiency and effectiveness of the project**: By managing quality and the team effectively, project managers can improve the efficiency and effectiveness of the project.

Compare Quality Management and Team Management

Quality management and team management tools and techniques can be used together to improve the performance of projects. However, there are some key differences between the two.

Quality management is the process of ensuring that the project meets or exceeds the requirements of the customer. Quality management tools and techniques can be used to identify, assess, and mitigate risks to the project's quality. Some common quality management tools and techniques include:

- Quality management plan
- Quality control procedures
- Quality assurance procedures
- Quality records
  Team management is the process of leading and motivating a team to achieve a common goal. Team management tools and techniques can be used to build and maintain a high-performing team.

Some common team management tools and techniques include:

- Team charter
- Team goals
- Team performance reviews
- Team communication plan

Comparison and contrast:

Characteristic	Quality management	Team management
Purpose	To ensure that the project meets or exceeds the requirements of the customer	To lead and motivate a team to achieve a common goal
Timeframe	Throughout the project lifecycle	Throughout the project lifecycle
Inputs	Project objectives, scope, and constraints	Project objectives, scope, constraints, and team members
Outputs	A quality management plan, quality control and quality assurance procedures, and quality records	A team charter, team goals, and team performance reviews
Key differences		
Focus	The quality of the project's deliverables	The performance and well-being of the team
Level of detail	More detailed	Less detailed

Examples of how quality management and team management tools and techniques can be used together:

- **Use team management tools and techniques to implement the quality management plan.** For example, the team charter can be used to define the team's roles and responsibilities for implementing quality control and quality assurance procedures. Team goals can be set to ensure that the team is focused on delivering high-quality deliverables.

- **Use quality management tools and techniques to monitor and improve team performance.** For example, quality control and quality assurance procedures can be used to identify and address team performance issues. Quality records can be used to track team performance over time and identify areas for improvement.

- **Use quality management and team management tools and techniques to create a culture of continuous improvement.** By focusing on both quality and team performance, organizations can create a culture where everyone is committed to delivering the best possible results.

Guidelines for using quality management and team management tools and techniques effectively:

- **Involve stakeholders in the development and implementation of quality management and team management plans.** This will help to ensure that everyone is on the same page and that the plans are aligned with the project's objectives.

- **Use data to drive decisions about quality management and team management.** This will help to ensure that the plans are effective and that resources are being allocated efficiently.

- **Be flexible and adaptable.** Things change, so be prepared to adjust quality management and team management plans as needed.

- **Communicate regularly with stakeholders about quality management and team management plans.** This will help to keep everyone informed and ensure that everyone is working towards the same goals.

- **Celebrate successes and recognize individual contributions.** This will help to motivate the team and maintain a positive team culture.

Quality management

- **Develop a quality management plan.** The quality management plan should define the project's quality objectives, the quality control and quality assurance procedures to be used, and the quality records to be maintained.

- **Implement quality control and quality assurance procedures.** Quality control procedures are used to identify and correct defects during the project lifecycle. Quality assurance procedures are used to assess the quality of the project's deliverables and ensure that they meet the quality objectives.

- **Maintain quality records.** Quality records provide evidence that the project's quality objectives have been met. Quality records can also be used to identify areas for improvement.

Team management

- **Develop a team charter.** The team charter should define the team's goals, roles and responsibilities, and communication plan.

- **Set team goals.** Team goals should be specific, measurable, achievable, relevant, and time-bound.

- **Conduct team performance reviews.** Team performance reviews should be used to assess the team's progress towards its goals and to identify areas for improvement.

- **Develop a team communication plan.** The team communication plan should define how the team will communicate with each other and with stakeholders.

Quality management tools and techniques help to ensure that the project meets or exceeds the requirements of the customer. Some common quality management tools and techniques include:

- **Quality management plan** - a document that defines the project's quality objectives, the quality control and quality assurance procedures to be used, and the quality records to be maintained.

- **Checklists** - used to verify that all necessary steps have been completed and that all requirements have been met.

- **Inspections** - used to identify and correct defects.

- **Testing** - used to evaluate the performance of the project's deliverables.

- **Statistical process control** - used to identify and monitor variations in the project's processes.

Team management tools and techniques help to lead and motivate a team to achieve a common goal. Some common team management tools and techniques include:

- **Team charter** - a document that defines the team's goals, roles and responsibilities, and communication plan.

- **Work breakdown structure** - a hierarchical decomposition of the work of the project into smaller and more manageable tasks.

- **Gantt chart** - a bar chart that shows the start and end dates of tasks, as well as the dependencies between tasks.

- **Risk management plan** - a document that identifies and assesses the risks to the project, and develops mitigation plans to reduce the impact of those risks.

- **Communication plan** - a document that identifies the communication needs of the project and defines how information will be communicated to stakeholders.

Part III: Emerging PM Tools and Techniques

Chapter 12: Business Intelligence and Data Analytics for Project Management

Business intelligence (BI) and data analytics are emerging PM tools and techniques that can help project managers to make better decisions, improve efficiency, and reduce risks.

Business intelligence is the process of collecting, analyzing, and visualizing data to inform business decisions. BI tools can help project managers to track project progress, identify potential problems, and make informed decisions about how to proceed.

Data analytics is the use of statistical methods and machine learning to extract insights from data. Data analytics can be used to identify patterns and trends, predict future events, and optimize project performance.

Here are some specific ways that BI and data analytics can be used for project management:

- **Track project progress**: BI tools can be used to track project progress in real time, including metrics such as task completion rates, budget spending, and schedule adherence. This information can help project managers to identify potential problems early and make necessary adjustments.

- **Identify potential problems**: BI tools can be used to identify potential problems with a project, such as tasks that are at risk of falling behind schedule or budget overruns. This information can help project managers to take corrective action before the problems become too serious.

- **Make informed decisions**: BI tools can provide project managers with the data they need to make informed decisions about how to proceed with a project. For example, project managers can use BI tools to compare different project plans or to assess the risk of different options.

- **Predict future events**: Data analytics can be used to predict future events, such as the likelihood of a project being completed on time and on budget. This information can help project managers to make better decisions about how to allocate resources and manage the project.

- **Optimize project performance**: Data analytics can be used to optimize project performance by identifying areas where efficiency can be improved. For example, data analytics can be used to identify tasks that are taking longer than expected or to identify bottlenecks in the project workflow.

Overall, BI and data analytics are powerful tools that can help project managers to be more successful. By using these tools, project managers can make better decisions, improve efficiency, and reduce risks.

Here are some additional tips for using BI and data analytics for project management:

- **Identify the right data to collect**: The first step is to identify the right data to collect for your project. This will depend on the specific needs of the project and the types of decisions that you need to make.

- **Clean and prepare the data**: Once you have collected the data, it is important to clean and prepare it for analysis. This may involve removing duplicate records, correcting errors, and formatting the data in a consistent way.

- **Use the right tools**: There are a variety of BI and data analytics tools available. Choose a tool that is right for the needs of your project and your team.

- **Get buy-in from stakeholders**: It is important to get buy-in from stakeholders for the use of BI and data analytics. This will help to ensure that everyone is on the same page and that the results of the analysis are accepted and used to make decisions.

- **Monitor and update the analysis**: The analysis should be monitored and updated regularly to ensure that it is still relevant and accurate.

Chapter 13: Artificial Intelligence and Machine Learning for Project Management

Artificial intelligence (AI) and machine learning (ML) are emerging PM tools and techniques that have the potential to revolutionize project management. AI and ML can be used to automate tasks, improve decision-making, and predict future outcomes.

Here are some specific ways that AI and ML can be used for project management:

- **Automate tasks**: AI and ML can be used to automate repetitive and time-consuming tasks, such as scheduling, budgeting, and risk management. This can free up project managers to focus on more strategic tasks.

- **Improve decision-making**: AI and ML can be used to analyze large amounts of data to identify patterns and trends that would be difficult or impossible for humans to spot. This information can help project managers to make better decisions about resource allocation, task prioritization, and risk mitigation.

- **Predict future outcomes**: AI and ML can be used to predict future outcomes, such as the likelihood of a project being completed on time and on budget. This information can help project managers to develop contingency plans and make necessary adjustments to the project plan.

Here are some examples of how AI and ML are already being used in project management:

- **Project scheduling**: AI and ML can be used to develop project schedules that are more realistic and efficient. For example, AI and ML can be used to identify potential bottlenecks and conflicts in the project schedule.

- **Budgeting**: AI and ML can be used to develop more accurate budgets for projects. For example, AI and ML can be used to predict the cost of resources and to identify potential cost overruns.

- **Risk management**: AI and ML can be used to identify and assess risks to projects. For example, AI and ML can be used to analyze historical data to identify common risks and to predict the likelihood of those risks occurring.

- **Resource allocation**: AI and ML can be used to allocate resources to projects in a more efficient and effective way. For example, AI and ML can be used to identify the best people for each task and to ensure that tasks are assigned evenly.

- **Task prioritization**: AI and ML can be used to prioritize tasks based on their importance and urgency. This can help project managers to focus on the most important tasks first.

Overall, AI and ML have the potential to revolutionize project management by automating tasks, improving decision-making, and predicting future outcomes. However, it is important to note that AI and

ML are still in their early stages of development and there is still much research to be done.

Here are some additional tips for using AI and ML for project management:

- **Start small**: Don't try to implement AI and ML for all aspects of your project at once. Start by identifying a few specific tasks that can be automated or improved with AI and ML.

- **Get buy-in from stakeholders**: It is important to get buy-in from stakeholders for the use of AI and ML. This will help to ensure that everyone is on the same page and that the results of the AI and ML are accepted and used to make decisions.

- **Monitor and update the AI and ML models**: AI and ML models should be monitored and updated regularly to ensure that they are still accurate and relevant.

- **Be aware of the limitations of AI and ML**: AI and ML are powerful tools, but they are not perfect. It is important to be aware of the limitations of AI and ML and to use them in conjunction with human judgment.

Chapter 14: Agile Project Management Tools and Techniques

Agile project management tools and techniques are a rapidly growing area of the project management toolbox. Agile is a flexible and iterative approach to project management that is designed to adapt to change and deliver value to customers early and often.

Here are some of the most popular agile project management tools and techniques:

- **Kanban**: Kanban is a visualization tool that helps teams to track their work and identify bottlenecks. Kanban boards are typically divided into three columns: to do, in progress, and done. Teams move tasks through the columns as they are worked on and completed.

- **Scrum**: Scrum is a framework for agile project management that is based on short iterative cycles called sprints. Sprints typically last two weeks, and teams work to deliver a working product increment at the end of each sprint.

- **Extreme Programming (XP)**: XP is a set of software development practices that are designed to improve the quality and speed of development. XP practices include pair programming, test-driven development, and continuous integration.

- **Lean**: Lean is a methodology that focuses on eliminating waste from processes. Lean principles can be applied to agile project management to improve efficiency and deliver value to customers more quickly.

Agile project management tools and techniques can be used to manage a wide variety of projects, from software development to product design to marketing campaigns. Agile is particularly well-suited for projects that are complex, uncertain, or rapidly changing.

Here are some of the benefits of using agile project management tools and techniques:

- **Increased flexibility and adaptability**: Agile project management tools and techniques are designed to help teams adapt to change and deliver value to customers early and often. This is especially important in today's rapidly changing business environment.

- **Improved collaboration and communication**: Agile project management tools and techniques promote collaboration and communication between team members and stakeholders. This can help to identify and resolve problems more quickly and effectively.

- **Higher quality products and services**: Agile project management tools and techniques help teams to focus on delivering high-quality products and services to customers. This is because agile teams are constantly testing and improving their work.

- **Increased customer satisfaction**: Agile project management tools and techniques can help to increase customer satisfaction by delivering value to customers early and often. Agile teams also regularly work with customers to get feedback and make sure that they are meeting their needs.

Overall, agile project management tools and techniques can help teams to be more efficient, effective, and customer-centric. However, it is important to note that agile is not a silver bullet. Agile teams still need to have the right skills, tools, and processes in place to be successful.

Here are some additional tips for using agile project management tools and techniques:

- **Start small**: Don't try to implement agile for all of your projects at once. Start by identifying a few projects that are a good fit for agile.

- **Get buy-in from stakeholders**: It is important to get buy-in from stakeholders for the use of agile. This will help to ensure that everyone is on the same page and that the team is supported.

- **Train your team**: Make sure that your team is trained on the agile tools and techniques that you will be using. This will help them to be more effective and efficient.

- **Be flexible and adaptable**: Agile is all about being flexible and adaptable. Don't be afraid to change your approach as needed.

Chapter 15: Hybrid Project Management Tools and Techniques

Hybrid project management tools and techniques combine elements of multiple project management methodologies, such as agile and waterfall. Hybrid project management is often used for projects that are complex, uncertain, or rapidly changing, but also require some of the structure and predictability of waterfall.

Here are some of the most popular hybrid project management tools and techniques:

- **Scrumban:** Scrumban is a hybrid project management methodology that combines elements of Scrum and Kanban. Scrumban teams typically hold regular Scrum planning and review meetings, but they use a Kanban board to track their work. This flexibility allows teams to adapt to change and deliver value to customers early and often, while still maintaining some of the structure of Scrum.

- **Water-Scrum-Fall:** Water-Scrum-Fall is a hybrid project management methodology that combines elements of waterfall and Scrum. Water-Scrum-Fall projects are typically divided into three phases: a waterfall planning phase, an agile development phase, and a waterfall closure phase. This approach allows teams to benefit from the structure and predictability of waterfall for the planning and closure phases, while also benefiting from the flexibility and adaptability of agile for the development phase.

- **Feature-Driven Development (FDD)**: FDD is a hybrid project management methodology that combines elements of waterfall and agile. FDD projects are typically divided into two-week iterations, and teams work to deliver a working feature increment at the end of each iteration. FDD also includes a number of other practices, such as domain modeling, feature modeling, and planning by feature.

Hybrid project management tools and techniques can be used to manage a wide variety of projects, from software development to product design to construction. Hybrid project management is particularly well-suited for projects that are complex, uncertain, or rapidly changing.

Here are some of the benefits of using hybrid project management tools and techniques:

- **Increased flexibility and adaptability**: Hybrid project management tools and techniques combine the flexibility and adaptability of agile with the structure and predictability of waterfall. This allows teams to adapt to change and deliver value to customers early and often, while still maintaining some control over the project.

- **Improved collaboration and communication**: Hybrid project management tools and techniques promote collaboration and communication between team members and stakeholders. This can help to identify and resolve problems more quickly and effectively.

- **Higher quality products and services**: Hybrid project management tools and techniques help teams to focus on delivering high-quality products and services to customers. This is because hybrid teams are constantly testing and improving their work.

- **Increased customer satisfaction**: Hybrid project management tools and techniques can help to increase customer satisfaction by delivering value to customers early and often. Hybrid teams also regularly work with customers to get feedback and make sure that they are meeting their needs.

Overall, hybrid project management tools and techniques can be a valuable tool for managing complex, uncertain, or rapidly changing projects. However, it is important to note that hybrid project management is not a silver bullet. Hybrid teams still need to have the right skills, tools, and processes in place to be successful.

Here are some additional tips for using hybrid project management tools and techniques:

- **Choose the right methodology**: There is no one-size-fits-all hybrid project management methodology. The best methodology for your project will depend on the specific needs of the project and the team.

- **Get buy-in from stakeholders**: It is important to get buy-in from stakeholders for the use of hybrid project management. This will help to ensure that everyone is on the same page and that the team is supported.

- **Train your team**: Make sure that your team is trained on the hybrid project management tools and techniques that you will be using. This will help them to be more effective and efficient.

- **Be flexible and adaptable**: Hybrid project management is all about being flexible and adaptable. Don't be afraid to change your approach as needed.

Part IV: Customizing and Adapting the PM Toolbox

Chapter 16: Selecting the Right Tools for Your Project

When selecting the right tools for your project, there are a number of factors to consider, including:

- **The size and complexity of your project**: Smaller and less complex projects may require fewer tools, while larger and more complex projects may require a more comprehensive set of tools.

- **The budget for your project**: Some tools are free or open source, while others can be expensive. It is important to choose tools that fit your budget.

- **The skills and experience of your team**: Some tools are more complex and require more training to use than others. It is important to choose tools that your team is comfortable using.

- **The specific needs of your project**: Different projects have different needs. For example, a software development project may require different tools than a marketing campaign.

Once you have considered these factors, you can start to evaluate different tools and choose the ones that are right for your project.

Here are some additional tips for selecting the right tools for your project:

- **Do your research**: Read reviews and compare different tools before making a decision.

- **Get feedback from your team**: Ask your team members what tools they are comfortable using and what features are important to them.

- **Start small**: You don't need to buy all of the tools you think you might need upfront. Start with a small set of tools and add more as needed.

- **Be flexible**: Things change, so be prepared to change your toolset as needed.

Customizing and adapting the PM toolbox

The PM toolbox is a collection of tools and techniques that can be used to manage projects. The toolbox is not one-size-fits-all, and it can be customized and adapted to meet the specific needs of each project.

Here are some tips for customizing and adapting the PM toolbox:

- **Identify the tools and techniques that are relevant to your project**: Not all of the tools and techniques in the PM toolbox will be relevant to every project. Identify the tools and techniques that are most relevant to your project and focus on those.

- **Add your own tools and techniques**: If there are tools or techniques that you are comfortable using and that you think would be helpful for your project, add them to the PM toolbox.

- **Adapt the tools and techniques to your project**: The tools and techniques in the PM toolbox can be adapted to meet the specific needs of your project. For example, you may need to modify the project management plan template to include additional information or to remove information that is not relevant to your project.

By customizing and adapting the PM toolbox, you can create a set of tools and techniques that is tailored to the specific needs of your project. This will help you to be more efficient and effective in managing your project.

Here are some additional tips for customizing and adapting the PM toolbox:

- **Get buy-in from stakeholders**: It is important to get buy-in from stakeholders for the customized PM toolbox. This will help to ensure that everyone is on the same page and that the toolbox is supported.

- **Train your team**: Make sure that your team is trained on the customized PM toolbox. This will help them to be more effective and efficient in using the tools and techniques.

- **Monitor and update the PM toolbox**: The PM toolbox should be monitored and updated regularly to ensure that it is still meeting the needs of the project.

Chapter 17: Integrating PM Tools and Systems

Integrating PM tools and systems can be a complex task, but it can also be very rewarding. When done correctly, integration can help to improve efficiency, reduce errors, and increase visibility.

There are a few different ways to integrate PM tools and systems. One common approach is to use a third-party integration tool. These tools can help to connect different PM tools and systems together, allowing data to flow seamlessly between them.

Another approach to integration is to use native integrations. Some PM tools and systems offer native integrations with other popular PM tools and systems. These integrations are typically easier to set up and use than third-party integration tools.

Finally, some PM tools and systems can be integrated using custom APIs. This approach is more complex and requires more technical expertise than the other two approaches, but it can offer more flexibility.

When choosing an integration approach, it is important to consider the following factors:

- **The specific PM tools and systems that you need to integrate**: Not all integration tools and systems are compatible with each other. It is important to choose an integration approach that is compatible with the specific PM tools and systems that you need to integrate.

- **Your budget**: Integration can be expensive. It is important to choose an integration approach that fits your budget.

- **Your technical expertise**: Some integration approaches are more complex than others. It is important to choose an integration approach that is appropriate for your technical expertise.

Customizing and adapting the PM toolbox

The PM toolbox can be customized and adapted to meet the specific needs of each project. This includes integrating PM tools and systems.

Here are some tips for customizing and adapting the PM toolbox to integrate PM tools and systems:

- **Identify the PM tools and systems that you need to integrate**: The first step is to identify the PM tools and systems that you need to integrate. This will depend on the specific needs of your project.

- **Choose an integration approach**: Once you have identified the PM tools and systems that you need to integrate, you need to choose an integration approach. As discussed above, there are three main integration approaches: third-party integration tools, native integrations, and custom APIs.

- **Implement the integration**: Once you have chosen an integration approach, you need to implement the integration.

This may involve configuring the integration tools or systems, or writing custom code.

- **Test the integration**: Once you have implemented the integration, you need to test it to make sure that it is working properly.

- **Monitor and update the integration**: The integration should be monitored and updated regularly to ensure that it is still working properly and meeting the needs of the project.

By following these tips, you can customize and adapt the PM toolbox to integrate PM tools and systems. This will help you to improve efficiency, reduce errors, and increase visibility.

Here are some additional tips for customizing and adapting the PM toolbox to integrate PM tools and systems:

- **Get buy-in from stakeholders**: It is important to get buy-in from stakeholders for the customized PM toolbox. This will help to ensure that everyone is on the same page and that the toolbox is supported.

- **Train your team**: Make sure that your team is trained on the customized PM toolbox and the integrated PM tools and systems. This will help them to be more effective and efficient in using the tools and systems.

- **Document the integration**: It is important to document the integration so that others can understand it and maintain it.

Chapter 18: Managing Change in the PM Toolbox

Change is inevitable in any project, and the PM toolbox is no exception. As the project's needs change, so too must the PM toolbox.

Here are some tips for managing change in the PM toolbox:

- **Identify the need for change**: The first step is to identify the need for change. This may be triggered by a change in the project's scope, budget, schedule, or team.

- **Assess the impact of the change**: Once you have identified the need for change, you need to assess the impact of the change on the project. This includes identifying the tools and techniques that will be affected by the change, as well as the impact on the project's schedule, budget, and team.

- **Develop a plan for change**: Once you have assessed the impact of the change, you need to develop a plan for change. This plan should identify the specific changes that need to be made, as well as the resources and timeline for implementing the changes.

- **Communicate the change**: Once you have developed a plan for change, you need to communicate the change to the project team and stakeholders. This is important to ensure that everyone is on the same page and that there are no surprises.

- **Implement the change**: Once you have communicated the change, you need to implement it. This may involve updating the PM plan, training the project team on new tools or techniques, or changing the project's schedule or budget.

- **Monitor and update the change**: Once you have implemented the change, you need to monitor it to ensure that it is working as intended. You may also need to update the change as needed.

Customizing and adapting the PM toolbox

The PM toolbox can be customized and adapted to meet the specific needs of each project. This includes managing change in the PM toolbox.

Here are some tips for customizing and adapting the PM toolbox to manage change:

- **Identify the types of changes that are likely to occur**: The first step is to identify the types of changes that are likely to occur on your project. This will help you to develop a plan for managing change.

- **Develop a process for managing change**: Once you have identified the types of changes that are likely to occur, you need to develop a process for managing change. This process should include steps for identifying, assessing, planning, communicating, implementing, and monitoring changes.

101

- **Use a change management tool**: There are a number of change management tools available that can help you to manage change in the PM toolbox. These tools can help you to track changes, assess the impact of changes, and communicate changes to the project team and stakeholders.

By following these tips, you can customize and adapt the PM toolbox to manage change effectively. This will help you to keep the PM toolbox up-to-date and relevant to the needs of the project.

Here are some additional tips for customizing and adapting the PM toolbox to manage change:

- **Get buy-in from stakeholders**: It is important to get buy-in from stakeholders for the change management process. This will help to ensure that everyone is on the same page and that the process is supported.

- **Train your team**: Make sure that your team is trained on the change management process. This will help them to be more effective in managing change.

- **Document the change management process**: It is important to document the change management process so that others can understand it and follow it.

Chapter 19: Continuously Improving the PM Toolbox

Continuous improvement is the process of making small, incremental changes to improve the PM toolbox over time. Continuous improvement can help to ensure that the PM toolbox is always up-to-date and meeting the needs of the project.

Here are some tips for continuously improving the PM toolbox:

- **Regularly review the PM toolbox**: The first step is to regularly review the PM toolbox. This will help you to identify areas where the toolbox can be improved.

- **Get feedback from the project team and stakeholders**: Ask the project team and stakeholders for feedback on the PM toolbox. This feedback can help you to identify areas where the toolbox can be improved.

- **Identify areas for improvement**: Once you have reviewed the PM toolbox and gathered feedback, you can identify areas where the toolbox can be improved. This may include adding new tools and techniques, removing outdated tools and techniques, or updating existing tools and techniques.

- **Make changes to the PM toolbox**: Once you have identified areas for improvement, you need to make changes to the PM toolbox. This may involve adding new tools and techniques, removing outdated tools and techniques, or updating existing tools and techniques.

- **Test the changes**: Once you have made changes to the PM toolbox, you need to test the changes to ensure that they are working as intended.

- **Monitor the changes**: Once you have tested the changes, you need to monitor the changes to ensure that they are having the desired effect.

Customizing and adapting the PM toolbox

The PM toolbox can be customized and adapted to meet the specific needs of each project. This includes continuously improving the PM toolbox.

Here are some tips for customizing and adapting the PM toolbox to continuously improve it:

- **Develop a process for continuous improvement**: The first step is to develop a process for continuous improvement. This process should include steps for reviewing the PM toolbox, gathering feedback, identifying areas for improvement, making changes to the PM toolbox, testing the changes, and monitoring the changes.

- **Use a continuous improvement tool**: There are a number of continuous improvement tools available that can help you to continuously improve the PM toolbox. These tools can help you to track changes, assess the impact of changes, and communicate changes to the project team and stakeholders.

- **Get buy-in from stakeholders**: It is important to get buy-in from stakeholders for the continuous improvement process. This will help to ensure that everyone is on the same page and that the process is supported.

- **Train your team**: Make sure that your team is trained on the continuous improvement process. This will help them to be more effective in continuously improving the PM toolbox.

- **Document the continuous improvement process**: It is important to document the continuous improvement process so that others can understand it and follow it.

By following these tips, you can customize and adapt the PM toolbox to continuously improve it. This will help you to keep the PM toolbox up-to-date, relevant, and efficient.

Here are some additional tips for customizing and adapting the PM toolbox to continuously improve it:

- **Be flexible**: The continuous improvement process should be flexible enough to adapt to the changing needs of the project.

- **Be persistent**: Continuous improvement is an ongoing process. Don't expect to make all of the necessary improvements at once. Just keep making small, incremental changes over time.

- **Celebrate successes**: It is important to celebrate successes along the way. This will help to motivate the team and keep them engaged in the continuous improvement process.

Additional

Project governance and compliance

Project governance and compliance are essential components of a successful project management toolbox. Project governance provides the framework for making decisions, managing risks, and ensuring that the project is aligned with the organization's overall goals and objectives. Compliance ensures that the project is meeting all applicable laws, regulations, and standards.

The project management toolbox should include tools and techniques to support both project governance and compliance. For example, a project governance tool might help the project manager to develop and track the project charter, project plan, and risk management plan. A compliance tool might help the project manager to track and manage compliance with all applicable laws, regulations, and standards.

Here are some specific examples of how project governance and compliance can be supported by the project management toolbox:

- **Project charter:** The project charter is a document that formally authorizes the project and defines its scope, goals, and objectives. The project management toolbox can include tools and templates to help the project manager develop and manage the project charter.

- **Project plan:** The project plan is a document that outlines the steps that need to be taken to achieve the project's goals and objectives. The project management toolbox can include tools and templates to help the project manager develop and manage the project plan.

- **Risk management plan:** The risk management plan is a document that identifies and assesses the risks to the project, and outlines mitigation strategies. The project management toolbox can include tools and techniques to help the project manager develop and manage the risk management plan.

- **Compliance matrix:** A compliance matrix is a document that identifies all applicable laws, regulations, and standards, and outlines how the project will comply with them. The project management toolbox can include tools and templates to help the project manager develop and manage the compliance matrix.

- **Audit checklist:** An audit checklist is a document that lists all of the items that need to be audited to ensure compliance with all applicable laws, regulations, and standards. The project management toolbox can include audit checklists for specific types of projects, such as software development projects or construction projects.

By using the project management toolbox to support project governance and compliance, project managers can help to ensure that their projects are successful and meet all applicable requirements.

Here are some additional tips for using the project management toolbox to support project governance and compliance:

- **Customize the project management toolbox to meet the specific needs of your project.** Not all projects require the same level of governance and compliance. Customize the project management toolbox to include the tools and techniques that are most relevant to your project.

- **Get buy-in from stakeholders.** It is important to get buy-in from all stakeholders for the project governance and compliance framework. This will help to ensure that everyone is on the same page and that the framework is supported.

- **Train your team.** Make sure that your team is trained on the project governance and compliance framework. This will help them to understand their roles and responsibilities, and to comply with the framework.

- **Monitor and update the project governance and compliance framework.** The project governance and compliance framework should be monitored and updated regularly to ensure that it is still effective and meeting the needs of the project.

Project sustainability

Project sustainability is the ability of a project to deliver lasting benefits to the organization and society. It is important to consider project sustainability at all stages of the project lifecycle, from planning to execution to closure.

The project management toolbox can include tools and techniques to support project sustainability. For example, a project sustainability assessment tool might help the project manager to identify and assess the social, environmental, and economic impacts of the project. A project sustainability management plan might help the project manager to develop and implement strategies to mitigate the negative impacts of the project and maximize the positive impacts.

Here are some specific examples of how project sustainability can be supported by the project management toolbox:

- **Project sustainability assessment:** A project sustainability assessment is a process of identifying and assessing the social, environmental, and economic impacts of a project. The project management toolbox can include tools and templates to help the project manager conduct a project sustainability assessment.

- **Project sustainability management plan:** A project sustainability management plan is a document that outlines the strategies that will be used to mitigate the negative impacts of the project and maximize the positive impacts. The project management toolbox can include tools and templates to help the project manager develop and manage a project sustainability management plan.

- **Green building standards:** Green building standards are a set of criteria that promote the design, construction, and operation of sustainable buildings. The project management toolbox can include tools and templates to help the project manager comply with green building standards.

- **Social impact assessment:** A social impact assessment is a process of identifying and assessing the social impacts of a project. The project management toolbox can include tools and templates to help the project manager conduct a social impact assessment.

- **Economic impact assessment:** An economic impact assessment is a process of identifying and assessing the economic impacts of a project. The project management toolbox can include tools and templates to help the project manager conduct an economic impact assessment.

By using the project management toolbox to support project sustainability, project managers can help to ensure that their projects deliver lasting benefits to the organization and society.

Here are some additional tips for using the project management toolbox to support project sustainability:

- **Customize the project management toolbox to meet the specific needs of your project.** Not all projects have the same sustainability challenges and opportunities. Customize the project management toolbox to include the tools and techniques that are most relevant to your project.

- **Get buy-in from stakeholders.** It is important to get buy-in from all stakeholders for the project sustainability framework. This will help to ensure that everyone is on the same page and that the framework is supported.

- **Train your team.** Make sure that your team is trained on the project sustainability framework. This will help them to understand their roles and responsibilities, and to contribute to the project's sustainability goals.

- **Monitor and update the project sustainability framework.** The project sustainability framework should be monitored and updated regularly to ensure that it is still effective and meeting the needs of the project.

Project resilience

Project resilience is the ability of a project to adapt to and recover from disruptions. Disruptions can come in many forms, such as natural disasters, economic downturns, or technological changes. Project resilience is important because it can help to ensure that projects are able to meet their goals and objectives, even in the face of disruptions.

The project management toolbox can include tools and techniques to support project resilience. For example, a risk management tool might help the project manager to identify and assess the risks to the project, and to develop mitigation strategies. A contingency planning tool might help the project manager to develop plans for responding to disruptions.

Here are some specific examples of how project resilience can be supported by the project management toolbox:

- **Risk management**: Risk management is the process of identifying, assessing, and mitigating the risks to a project. The project management toolbox can include tools and techniques to help the project manager develop and implement a risk management plan.

- **Contingency planning**: Contingency planning is the process of developing plans for responding to disruptions. The project management toolbox can include tools and templates to help the project manager develop and manage contingency plans.

- **Scenario planning**: Scenario planning is the process of developing plans for responding to different possible future scenarios. The project management toolbox can include tools and templates to help the project manager develop and manage scenario plans.

- **Resilience assessment**: A resilience assessment is a process of evaluating the resilience of a project to disruptions. The project management toolbox can include tools and templates to help the project manager conduct a resilience assessment.

- **Resilience management plan**: A resilience management plan is a document that outlines the strategies that will be used to improve the resilience of the project. The project management toolbox can include tools and templates to help the project manager develop and manage a resilience management plan.

By using the project management toolbox to support project resilience, project managers can help to ensure that their projects are able to adapt to and recover from disruptions.

Here are some additional tips for using the project management toolbox to support project resilience:

- **Customize the project management toolbox to meet the specific needs of your project.** Not all projects have the same resilience challenges and opportunities. Customize the project management toolbox to include the tools and techniques that are most relevant to your project.

- **Get buy-in from stakeholders.** It is important to get buy-in from all stakeholders for the project resilience framework. This will help to ensure that everyone is on the same page and that the framework is supported.

- **Train your team.** Make sure that your team is trained on the project resilience framework. This will help them to understand their roles and responsibilities, and to contribute to the project's resilience goals.

- **Monitor and update the project resilience framework.** The project resilience framework should be monitored and updated regularly to ensure that it is still effective and meeting the needs of the project.

Project diversity and inclusion

Project diversity and inclusion is the practice of creating a project team and environment that is inclusive of people of all backgrounds, identities, and experiences. This includes diversity in terms of race, ethnicity, gender, sexual orientation, age, disability, religion, socioeconomic status, and more.

A diverse and inclusive project team can bring a wider range of perspectives and ideas to the table, which can lead to better decision-making and more innovative solutions. Additionally, a diverse and inclusive work environment can help to create a sense of belonging and engagement for all team members, which can lead to improved productivity and morale.

The project management toolbox can include tools and techniques to support project diversity and inclusion. For example, an unconscious bias training tool might help project managers to identify and mitigate their own unconscious biases. A diversity and inclusion checklist might help project managers to ensure that their project team is diverse and inclusive.

Here are some specific examples of how project diversity and inclusion can be supported by the project management toolbox:

- **Unconscious bias training:** Unconscious bias training is a process of helping people to identify and mitigate their own unconscious biases. The project management toolbox can include unconscious bias training tools to help project managers and their teams to become more aware of their own biases and to make more objective decisions.

- **Diversity and inclusion checklist:** A diversity and inclusion checklist is a document that lists all of the things that a project manager can do to create a diverse and inclusive project team and environment. The project management toolbox can include diversity and inclusion checklists for specific types of projects, such as software development projects or construction projects.

- **Diversity and inclusion goals:** Diversity and inclusion goals are specific targets that a project manager can set for their team. For example, a diversity and inclusion goal might be to increase the percentage of women on the project team to 50%. The project management toolbox can include tools and templates to help project managers to develop and track diversity and inclusion goals.

- **Diversity and inclusion training:** Diversity and inclusion training is a process of teaching people about the importance of diversity and inclusion and how to create a more diverse and inclusive workplace. The project management toolbox can include diversity and inclusion training tools to help project managers and their teams to learn more about diversity and inclusion and to develop the skills needed to create a more inclusive work environment.

By using the project management toolbox to support project diversity and inclusion, project managers can help to create more diverse and inclusive workplaces, which can lead to better decision-making, more innovative solutions, and improved productivity and morale.

Here are some additional tips for using the project management toolbox to support project diversity and inclusion:

- **Customize the project management toolbox to meet the specific needs of your project.** Not all projects have the same diversity and inclusion challenges and opportunities. Customize the project management toolbox to include the tools and techniques that are most relevant to your project.

- **Get buy-in from stakeholders.** It is important to get buy-in from all stakeholders for the project diversity and inclusion framework. This will help to ensure that everyone is on the same page and that the framework is supported.

- **Train your team.** Make sure that your team is trained on the project diversity and inclusion framework. This will help them to understand their roles and responsibilities, and to contribute to the project's diversity and inclusion goals.

- **Monitor and update the project diversity and inclusion framework.** The project diversity and inclusion framework should be monitored and updated regularly to ensure that it is still effective and meeting the needs of the project.

The Toolbox

Work Breakdown Structure (WBS)

A work breakdown structure (WBS) is a hierarchical decomposition of the work of a project into smaller and more manageable components. It is a tree diagram that shows the relationship between the project's deliverables and the tasks that need to be completed to produce them.

The WBS is typically created at the beginning of the project, but it can be updated throughout the project lifecycle as needed. It is an important tool for project planning and management, as it helps to ensure that all of the work required to complete the project is identified, estimated, and scheduled.

Creating a WBS

The following are the steps to create a WBS:

1. **Identify the project's main deliverables.** What are the products or services that the project will produce?

2. **Break down each deliverable into smaller and more manageable components.** Continue breaking down the components until you reach a level of detail that is appropriate for your project.

3. **Organize the components in a hierarchical structure, with the highest-level components at the top and the lowest-level**

components at the bottom. The highest-level component should be the project itself.

4. **Assign a unique identifier to each component.** This will help you to track progress and monitor costs.

Example of a WBS

The following is an example of a WBS for a software development project:

Project: Develop and launch a new mobile app

Deliverables:
- Mobile app for iOS and Android devices
- Server-side backend
- Documentation

Mobile app:
- Design and development
  - User interface design
  - User experience design
  - Front-end development
  - Back-end development
- Testing
  - Unit testing
  - Integration testing
  - System testing
  - User acceptance testing
- Deployment
  - App Store deployment
  - Google Play deployment

Server-side backend:
- Design and development
  - Database design
  - API design
  - Implementation
- Testing
  - Unit testing
  - Integration testing
  - System testing
- Deployment
  - Cloud deployment

Documentation:
- User guide
- Technical documentation

Benefits of using a WBS

A WBS offers a number of benefits, including:

- **It helps to ensure that all of the work required to complete the project is identified and accounted for.** This can help to prevent scope creep and ensure that the project is completed on time and within budget.

- **It breaks down the project into smaller and more manageable tasks.** This makes it easier to estimate and schedule the work, as well as to track progress and identify potential problems early on.

- **It helps to identify dependencies between tasks.** This ensures that the project is scheduled in a logical order and that tasks are not started before their dependencies are completed.

- **It provides a common framework for communication and collaboration between team members.** Everyone involved in the project can use the WBS to understand their roles and responsibilities, as well as the overall progress of the project.

- **It can be used to track progress and identify areas where the project is at risk of going over budget or behind schedule.** This allows project managers to take corrective action early on and avoid major problems.

A work breakdown structure (WBS) is a hierarchical decomposition of the work of a project into smaller and more manageable components. It is a tree diagram that shows the relationship between the project's deliverables and the tasks that need to be completed to produce them.

Here is a comparison and contrast of WBS with other project management tools and techniques:

WBS vs. Project Charter

A project charter is a document that defines the project's objectives, scope, constraints, and assumptions. It is typically created at the beginning of the project and used to guide the project team throughout the project lifecycle.

The WBS is a more detailed tool than the project charter. It breaks down the project's work into smaller and more manageable tasks, and it shows the relationship between the tasks. The WBS can be used to create a project schedule, estimate the cost of the project, and track progress.

WBS vs. Stakeholder Register

A stakeholder register is a document that identifies all of the stakeholders in a project, their interests in the project, and their level of influence over the project. It is used to manage stakeholder expectations and ensure that all stakeholders are kept informed of the project's progress.

The WBS is not a stakeholder management tool. However, it can be used to identify the stakeholders who are responsible for each task in the project. This information can be used to create a stakeholder communication plan and to ensure that the right stakeholders are involved in the project at the right time.

WBS vs. Risk Register

A risk register is a document that identifies all of the risks to a project, their likelihood, and their impact. It is used to develop risk mitigation strategies and to track the progress of those strategies.

The WBS can be used to identify the risks associated with each task in the project. This information can be used to update the risk register and to develop risk mitigation strategies.

WBS vs. Project Schedule

A project schedule is a timeline that shows the start and end dates of each task in the project, as well as the dependencies between the tasks. It is used to track the progress of the project and to identify potential problems early on.

The WBS is used to create the project schedule. It provides a breakdown of the project's work into smaller and more manageable tasks, which makes it easier to estimate the duration of each task and to create a realistic schedule.

Guidelines for creating a WBS:

- **Be clear about the project's objectives.** What are the products or services that the project will produce?

- **Identify all of the deliverables that are required to achieve the project's objectives.**

- **Break down each deliverable into smaller and more manageable components.** Continue breaking down the components until you reach a level of detail that is appropriate for your project.

- **Organize the components in a hierarchical structure, with the highest-level components at the top and the lowest-level components at the bottom.**

- **Assign a unique identifier to each component.** This will help you to track progress and monitor costs.

- **Involve the project team in the creation of the WBS.** This will help to ensure that the WBS is accurate and complete, and that everyone understands their roles and responsibilities.

- **Review and update the WBS regularly as the project progresses.** This will ensure that the WBS remains accurate and reflects the current state of the project.

Framework for using a WBS:

- **Use the WBS to create a project schedule.** Estimate the duration of each task in the WBS, and then sequence the tasks in a logical order.

- **Use the WBS to estimate the cost of the project.** Estimate the resources required for each task in the WBS, and then calculate the total cost of the project.

- **Use the WBS to track progress.** Track the completion of each task in the WBS, and then calculate the overall progress of the project.

- **Use the WBS to communicate with stakeholders.** Use the WBS to explain the project's scope and progress to stakeholders.

Best practices for using a WBS:

- **Use the WBS as a planning tool.** The WBS should be used to plan the project, not to track its progress.

- **Keep the WBS up-to-date.** The WBS should be reviewed and updated regularly as the project progresses.

- **Use the WBS as a communication tool.** The WBS can be used to communicate the project's scope and progress to stakeholders.

- **Use the WBS to manage risks.** The WBS can be used to identify and assess the risks associated with each task in the project.

Principles of WBS

- **Completeness:** The WBS must include all of the work that is required to complete the project.

- **Exclusivity**: Each work item in the WBS should be unique and not overlap with any other work items.

- **Arrangement**: The work items in the WBS should be arranged in a logical manner, such as by deliverable, phase, or function.

- **Decomposition**: The work items in the WBS should be decomposed into smaller and more manageable work items until the desired level of detail is reached.

Corollaries of WBS

- **100% rule**: The WBS must account for 100% of the project's work.

- **80/20 rule**: 80% of the project's effort is typically spent on 20% of the work items in the WBS.

- **10/90 rule**: The first 10% of the project's effort is typically spent on defining the WBS.

- **Scope creep**: Scope creep occurs when the project's scope is increased without a corresponding increase in the project's budget or schedule. This can be caused by changes in the project's requirements, or by the addition of new features or deliverables.

Syndromes of WBS

- **Gold-plating**: Gold-plating occurs when the project team exceeds the requirements of the project. This can lead to scope creep and increased costs.

- **Perfectionism**: Perfectionism occurs when the project team strives for perfection, even when it is not necessary. This can lead to delays and increased costs.

- **Analysis paralysis**: Analysis paralysis occurs when the project team spends too much time analyzing the project and not enough time taking action. This can lead to delays and increased costs.

Gantt Chart

A Gantt chart is a horizontal bar chart that shows the start and end dates of tasks, as well as the dependencies between tasks. It is a popular project management tool that can be used to plan, schedule, and track projects of all sizes.

Gantt charts are typically created using project management software, but they can also be created manually using a spreadsheet or whiteboard.

How to create a Gantt chart

To create a Gantt chart, follow these steps:

1. **Identify all of the tasks that need to be completed to complete the project.**

2. Estimate the duration of each task.

3. Sequence the tasks in a logical order, taking into account the dependencies between tasks.

4. Create a table or spreadsheet with two columns: one for the task name and one for the task duration.

5. Draw a horizontal bar for each task in the table or spreadsheet.

6. Position the bars on the timeline, taking into account the start and end dates of each task.

7. Add dependencies between tasks by drawing lines between the bars.

Example of a Gantt chart

The following is an example of a Gantt chart for a software development project:

Task	Duration (days)	Start date	End date
Requirements gathering	10	2023-11-07	2023-11-16
System design	15	2023-11-17	2023-12-01
Implementation	20	2023-12-02	2023-12-22
Testing	10	2023-12-23	2023-12-30
Deployment	5	2023-12-31	2023-01-05

Benefits of using a Gantt chart

Gantt charts offer a number of benefits, including:

- **They provide a visual overview of the project plan.** This can help project managers to identify potential problems and conflicts early on.

- **They can be used to track progress and identify delays.** This allows project managers to take corrective action early on.

- **They can be used to communicate the project plan to stakeholders.** This can help to ensure that everyone is on the same page and that everyone understands their roles and responsibilities.

Tips for using a Gantt chart

Here are some tips for using a Gantt chart:

- Be realistic when estimating the duration of tasks. It is better to overestimate the duration of tasks than to underestimate them.

- Keep the Gantt chart up-to-date as the project progresses. This will help to ensure that the Gantt chart remains accurate and reflects the current state of the project.

- Use dependencies to show the relationships between tasks. This will help to identify potential problems and conflicts early on.

- Communicate the Gantt chart to stakeholders. This will help to ensure that everyone is on the same page and that everyone understands their roles and responsibilities.

Gantt charts and PERT charts are both project management tools that can be used to visualize and track project progress. However, there are some key differences between the two.

Gantt charts

Gantt charts are horizontal bar charts that show the start and end dates of tasks, as well as the dependencies between tasks. They are a popular tool for project planning and scheduling, as they provide a clear and concise overview of the project timeline.

PERT charts

PERT charts are network diagrams that show the tasks involved in a project and their dependencies. They are a more complex tool than Gantt charts, but they can be more useful for projects with complex dependencies.

Comparison table

Feature	Gantt chart	PERT chart
Type of chart	Horizontal bar chart	Network diagram
Purpose	Project planning and scheduling	Project planning and risk management
Focus	Tasks and dependencies	Tasks and dependencies, as well as risk
Level of detail	Less detailed	More detailed
Complexity	Less complex	More complex

When to use a Gantt chart

Gantt charts are best suited for projects with simple dependencies and straightforward timelines. They are also a good choice for projects where communication with stakeholders is important, as they are easy to understand and interpret.

When to use a PERT chart

PERT charts are best suited for projects with complex dependencies and uncertain timelines. They are also a good choice for projects where risk management is important, as they can be used to identify and assess risks.

Which one is right for you?

The best project management tool for you will depend on the specific needs of your project. If you have a simple project with straightforward dependencies, a Gantt chart is a good choice. If you have a complex project with uncertain timelines or risk management is important, a PERT chart is a better choice.

You can also use both Gantt and PERT charts together. For example, you could use a PERT chart to plan the project and identify risks, and then use a Gantt chart to track progress and manage dependencies.

Ultimately, the best way to choose the right project management tool is to consider the specific needs of your project and your team.

Guidelines for creating a Gantt chart:

- Identify all of the tasks that need to be completed to complete the project.

- Estimate the duration of each task.

- Sequence the tasks in a logical order, taking into account the dependencies between tasks.

- Create a table or spreadsheet with two columns: one for the task name and one for the task duration.

- Draw a horizontal bar for each task in the table or spreadsheet.

- Position the bars on the timeline, taking into account the start and end dates of each task.
- Add dependencies between tasks by drawing lines between the bars.

Framework for using a Gantt chart:

- **Use the Gantt chart to plan the project.** The Gantt chart can help you to identify potential problems and conflicts early on.

- **Use the Gantt chart to track progress and identify delays.** The Gantt chart can help you to identify tasks that are behind schedule and to take corrective action.

- **Use the Gantt chart to communicate the project plan to stakeholders.** The Gantt chart can help to ensure that everyone is on the same page and that everyone understands their roles and responsibilities.

Best practices for using a Gantt chart:

- **Keep the Gantt chart up-to-date as the project progresses.** This will help to ensure that the Gantt chart remains accurate and reflects the current state of the project.

- **Use the Gantt chart to identify and assess risks.** The Gantt chart can help you to identify tasks that are at risk of delay or failure.

- **Use the Gantt chart to make informed decisions about the project.** The Gantt chart can help you to decide which tasks to prioritize and where to allocate resources.

Additional tips:

- Use color coding to highlight different aspects of the Gantt chart, such as task status, priority, or risk level.

- Add milestones to the Gantt chart to track key progress markers.

- Use the Gantt chart to create a project budget by estimating the cost of each task.

- Share the Gantt chart with stakeholders so that everyone is aligned on the project plan.

Principles of a Gantt chart

Completeness: The Gantt chart must include all of the work that is required to complete the project.

Exclusivity: Each work item in the Gantt chart should be unique and not overlap with any other work items.

Arrangement: The work items in the Gantt chart should be arranged in a logical manner, such as by deliverable, phase, or function.

Decomposition: The work items in the Gantt chart should be decomposed into smaller and more manageable work items until the desired level of detail is reached.

Corollaries of a Gantt chart

100% rule: The Gantt chart must account for 100% of the project's work.

80/20 rule: 80% of the project's effort is typically spent on 20% of the work items in the Gantt chart.

10/90 rule: The first 10% of the project's effort is typically spent on defining the Gantt chart.

Scope creep: Scope creep occurs when the project's scope is increased without a corresponding increase in the project's budget or schedule. This can be caused by changes in the project's requirements, or by the addition of new features or deliverables.

Syndromes of a Gantt chart

Gold-plating: Gold-plating occurs when the project team exceeds the requirements of the project. This can lead to scope creep and increased costs.

Perfectionism: Perfectionism occurs when the project team strives for perfection, even when it is not necessary. This can lead to delays and increased costs.

Analysis paralysis: Analysis paralysis occurs when the project team spends too much time analyzing the project and not enough time taking action. This can lead to delays and increased costs.

By understanding the principles, corollaries, and syndromes of a Gantt chart, project managers can avoid these pitfalls and create a Gantt chart that will help them to complete their projects on time, within budget, and to the required quality standards.

Here are some additional tips for using a Gantt chart effectively:

- Keep the Gantt chart up-to-date as the project progresses.

- Use realistic estimates for the duration of each task.

- Break down large tasks into smaller, more manageable tasks.

- Identify and manage dependencies between tasks.

- Use the Gantt chart to communicate the project plan to stakeholders.

Program Evaluation and Review Techniques (PERT)

Program Evaluation and Review Technique (PERT) is a project management tool used to estimate the time required to complete a project and to identify the critical path of the project. The critical path is the sequence of tasks that must be completed on time in order for the project to be completed on time.

PERT was developed by the US Navy in the 1950s to manage the Polaris missile program. It has since been widely adopted by project managers in a variety of industries.

PERT is a probabilistic method, which means that it takes into account the uncertainty in the duration of each task in the project. To do this, PERT uses three different time estimates for each task:

- **Optimistic estimate:** This is the shortest possible amount of time that the task could take under ideal conditions.

- **Most likely estimate:** This is the most realistic estimate of how long the task will take.

- **Pessimistic estimate:** This is the longest possible amount of time that the task could take under the worst possible conditions.

Once the time estimates have been made, PERT calculates the expected duration and variance of each task using the following formulas:

Expected duration:

Expected duration = (optimistic estimate + 4 * most likely estimate + pessimistic estimate) / 6

Variance:

Variance = (pessimistic estimate - optimistic estimate)^2 / 36

The expected duration and variance of the tasks in the project can then be used to calculate the expected duration and variance of the entire project.

PERT can be used to create a PERT chart, which is a visual representation of the project schedule and dependencies. PERT charts can be used to identify the critical path of the project, to track progress, and to manage change.

Benefits of using PERT

There are a number of benefits to using PERT, including:

- **Improved accuracy of project estimates:** PERT takes into account the uncertainty in the duration of each task, which can lead to more accurate project estimates.

- **Reduced risk of project delays:** PERT can be used to identify the critical path of the project, which allows project managers to focus their attention on the tasks that are most important for completing the project on time.

- **Improved communication and collaboration:** PERT charts can be used to communicate the project schedule and dependencies to stakeholders, which can improve communication and collaboration.

- **Enhanced project management skills**: Using PERT can help project managers to develop their project management skills, such as planning, scheduling, and risk management.

How to use PERT

To use PERT, follow these steps:

1. Identify all of the tasks in the project.

2. Estimate the optimistic, most likely, and pessimistic time estimates for each task.

3. Calculate the expected duration and variance of each task using the formulas above.

4. Calculate the expected duration and variance of the entire project.

5. Identify the critical path of the project.

6. Develop mitigation strategies for reducing the risk of the project.

7. Track progress and manage change.

Program Evaluation and Review Technique (PERT) and Critical Path Method (CPM) are two project management tools used to estimate the time required to complete a project and to identify the critical path of the project. The critical path is the sequence of tasks that must be completed on time in order for the project to be completed on time.

Here is a comparison and contrast of PERT and CPM:

Feature	PERT	CPM
Type of technique	Probabilistic	Deterministic
Time estimates	Three time estimates (optimistic, most likely, pessimistic)	One time estimate for each task
Critical path	Yes	Yes
Risk management	Yes	Limited
Complexity	More complex	Less complex

PERT is a more complex tool than CPM, but it is also more flexible and can be used to estimate the time required to complete projects with uncertain task durations. CPM is a less complex tool, but it is less flexible and can only be used to estimate the time required to complete projects with known task durations.

Here are some additional guidelines for choosing between PERT and CPM:

- **Use PERT for projects with uncertain task durations.** PERT is a good choice for projects where the duration of each task is difficult to estimate, such as research and development projects.

- **Use CPM for projects with known task durations.** CPM is a good choice for projects where the duration of each task is known, such as construction projects.

- **Use PERT for projects with a high degree of risk.** PERT is a good choice for projects where there is a high degree of risk, such as projects that are new or innovative.

- **Use CPM for projects with a low degree of risk.** CPM is a good choice for projects where there is a low degree of risk, such as projects that are routine or repetitive.

Guidelines for using Program Evaluation and Review Technique (PERT)

- **Identify all of the tasks in the project.**

- **Estimate the optimistic, most likely, and pessimistic time estimates for each task.**

- **Calculate the expected duration and variance of each task using the following formulas:**

    o Expected duration = (optimistic estimate + 4 * most likely estimate + pessimistic estimate) / 6

    o Variance = (pessimistic estimate - optimistic estimate)^2 / 36

- **Calculate the expected duration and variance of the entire project.**

- **Identify the critical path of the project.**

- **Develop mitigation strategies for reducing the risk of the project.**

- **Track progress and manage change.**

141

Framework for using PERT

PERT can be used to create a PERT chart, which is a visual representation of the project schedule and dependencies. PERT charts can be used to communicate the project plan to stakeholders, to track progress, and to manage change.

Tips for using PERT

- **Involve the project team in the process of estimating task durations.** This will help to ensure that the estimates are realistic and that everyone is on the same page.

- **Keep the PERT chart up-to-date as the project progresses.** This will help to ensure that the project is on track and that any potential problems can be identified and addressed early on.

- **Use PERT charts to communicate the project plan to stakeholders.** This will help to ensure that everyone is aligned on the project's goals and objectives.

Benefits of using PERT

There are a number of benefits to using PERT, including:

- **Improved accuracy of project estimates**: PERT takes into account the uncertainty in the duration of each task, which can lead to more accurate project estimates.

- **Reduced risk of project delays**: PERT can be used to identify the critical path of the project, which allows project managers to focus their attention on the tasks that are most important for completing the project on time.

- **Improved communication and collaboration**: PERT charts can be used to communicate the project schedule and dependencies to stakeholders, which can improve communication and collaboration.

- **Enhanced project management skills**: Using PERT can help project managers to develop their project management skills, such as planning, scheduling, and risk management.

Principles of Program Evaluation and Review Technique (PERT)

- **Completeness**: PERT includes all of the tasks and activities required to complete a project.

- **Exclusivity**: Each task in PERT is unique and does not overlap with any other task.

- **Arrangement**: Tasks in PERT are arranged in a logical order, with dependencies between tasks clearly identified.

- **Decomposition**: Tasks in PERT are decomposed into smaller and more manageable tasks until a desired level of detail is reached.

- **Probability**: PERT takes into account the uncertainty in the duration of each task by using probabilistic estimates.

Corollaries of PERT

- **100% Rule**: PERT accounts for 100% of the project's work.

- **80/20 Rule**: 80% of the project's effort is typically spent on 20% of the tasks.

- **10/90 Rule**: The first 10% of the project's effort is typically spent on defining the PERT chart.

- **Scope Creep**: Scope creep is the unplanned addition of new features or requirements to a project, which can lead to delays and increased costs.

Syndromes of PERT

- **Gold Plating**: Gold plating is the tendency to exceed the requirements of a project, which can lead to delays and increased costs.

- **Perfectionism**: Perfectionism is the tendency to strive for perfection, even when it is not necessary, which can lead to delays and increased costs.

- **Analysis Paralysis**: Analysis paralysis is the tendency to spend too much time analyzing a project and not enough time taking action, which can lead to delays and increased costs.

By understanding the principles, corollaries, and syndromes of PERT, project managers can avoid these pitfalls and use PERT to improve their project management skills and increase their chances of success.

Here are some additional tips for using PERT effectively:

- Keep the PERT chart up-to-date as the project progresses.

- Use realistic estimates for the duration of each task.

- Break down large tasks into smaller, more manageable tasks.

- Identify and manage dependencies between tasks.
- Use the PERT chart to communicate the project plan to stakeholders.

Earned Value Management (EVM)

Earned Value Management (EVM) is a project management methodology that integrates cost, schedule, and scope to measure project performance. It is based on the principle that the best way to predict the future is to understand the past.

EVM works by tracking three key metrics:

- **Planned Value (PV):** The budget for the work that has been scheduled to be completed by a certain date.

- **Actual Cost (AC):** The actual cost of the work that has been completed by a certain date.

- **Earned Value (EV):** The value of the work that has been completed by a certain date, based on the project's budget and schedule.

EVM calculates three key performance indicators (KPIs) based on these metrics:

- **Schedule Performance Index (SPI):** SPI = EV / PV. A SPI of 1.0 indicates that the project is on schedule. An SPI of less than 1.0 indicates that the project is behind schedule. An SPI of greater than 1.0 indicates that the project is ahead of schedule.

- **Cost Performance Index (CPI):** CPI = EV / AC. A CPI of 1.0 indicates that the project is within budget. A CPI of less than 1.0

indicates that the project is over budget. A CPI of greater than 1.0 indicates that the project is under budget.

- **Variance at Completion (VAC)**: VAC = Final PV - Final EV. VAC is a measure of how much the project is expected to cost over or under budget at completion. A positive VAC indicates that the project is expected to finish under budget. A negative VAC indicates that the project is expected to finish over budget.

Project managers can use EVM to track progress, identify problems early on, and take corrective action as needed. EVM can also be used to forecast the final cost and schedule of the project.

Benefits of using EVM

There are a number of benefits to using EVM, including:

- Improved project visibility: EVM provides project managers with a clear and concise view of project performance.

- Early identification of problems: EVM can help project managers to identify problems early on, when they are still relatively easy to fix.

- Informed decision-making: EVM can help project managers to make informed decisions about how to allocate resources and manage change.

- Increased stakeholder confidence: EVM can help to increase stakeholder confidence in the project by demonstrating that the project is being managed effectively.

How to use EVM

To use EVM, project managers need to:

1. Establish a baseline plan. This includes developing a project schedule and budget.

2. Track progress against the baseline plan. This involves tracking the actual cost and completion of work.

3. Calculate the EVM metrics. This involves calculating the PV, AC, EV, SPI, CPI, and VAC.

4. Analyze the EVM metrics. This involves comparing the EVM metrics to the baseline plan and to each other to identify trends and patterns.

5. Take corrective action. This involves taking action to address any problems that have been identified.

EVM can be a complex tool, but it can be very effective for improving project performance. Project managers who are interested in using EVM should consider taking a training course or hiring a consultant to help them get started.

Example

The following is an example of how EVM can be used to track project progress:

A project manager is tracking the progress of a software development project using EVM. The baseline plan for the project is as follows:

- Planned Value (PV): $100,000

- Schedule Performance Index (SPI): 1.0

The project manager tracks the actual cost and completion of work for the project. After two weeks, the project manager has the following data:

- Actual Cost (AC): $20,000

- Earned Value (EV): $25,000

The project manager can then calculate the following EVM metrics:

- SPI = EV / PV = $25,000 / $100,000 = 0.25

- CPI = EV / AC = $25,000 / $20,000 = 1.25

The project manager can then analyze the EVM metrics to identify trends and patterns. In this case, the SPI indicates that the project is behind schedule. The CPI indicates that the project is under budget.

The project manager can then take corrective action to address the problem of the project being behind schedule. For example, the project manager could allocate more resources to the project or reduce the scope of the project.

Comparison of EVM and other project management methodologies

Feature	EVM	Other project management methodologies
Type of methodology	Quantitative	Qualitative and quantitative
Focus	Cost, schedule, and scope	Cost, schedule, scope, quality, and risk
Complexity	More complex	Less complex
Data requirements	More data required	Less data required
Flexibility	Less flexible	More flexible

EVM is a more complex tool than other project management methodologies, but it is also more comprehensive and can provide more detailed insights into project performance. EVM is a good choice for projects where cost, schedule, and scope are critical factors.

Contrast of EVM and other project management methodologies

Feature	EVM	Other project management methodologies
Goal	To measure and forecast project performance	To plan, execute, and monitor projects
Tools used	EVM metrics, such as SPI, CPI, and VAC	Gantt charts, PERT charts, and risk registers
Benefits	Improved project visibility, early identification of problems, informed decision-making, and increased stakeholder confidence	Improved project planning, execution, and monitoring
Limitations	Complex to implement and use, requires a lot of data	Less comprehensive than EVM, may not provide all the insights needed to manage complex projects

Guidelines for using Earned Value Management (EVM) in project management

- **Establish a baseline plan.** This includes developing a project schedule and budget.

- **Track progress against the baseline plan.** This involves tracking the actual cost and completion of work.

- **Calculate the EVM metrics.** This involves calculating the PV, AC, EV, SPI, CPI, and VAC.

- **Analyze the EVM metrics.** This involves comparing the EVM metrics to the baseline plan and to each other to identify trends and patterns.

- **Take corrective action.** This involves taking action to address any problems that have been identified.

Framework for using EVM in project management

The following is a framework for using EVM in project management:

1. **Define the project scope.** This includes identifying all of the work that needs to be completed in order to complete the project.

2. **Develop a project schedule.** This involves breaking down the project scope into smaller tasks and estimating the duration of each task.

3. **Develop a project budget.** This involves estimating the cost of each task and summing the costs to calculate the total project budget.

4. **Implement the project.** This involves executing the tasks on the project schedule and tracking the actual cost and completion of work.

5. **Monitor project performance using EVM.** This involves calculating the EVM metrics and analyzing them to identify trends and patterns.

6. **Take corrective action to address any problems that have been identified.**

7. **Repeat steps 5 and 6 until the project is completed.**

Tips for using EVM effectively

- **Get buy-in from stakeholders.** It is important to get buy-in from stakeholders before implementing EVM. This will help to ensure that everyone is committed to using EVM and that everyone understands the benefits of using EVM.

- **Train the project team.** The project team needs to be trained on how to use EVM. This will help to ensure that the EVM data is accurate and reliable.

- **Use EVM consistently.** EVM should be used consistently throughout the project lifecycle. This will help to ensure that the EVM data is comparable over time.

- **Communicate the EVM results to stakeholders.** The EVM results should be communicated to stakeholders on a regular basis. This will help to keep stakeholders informed of the project's progress and to identify any potential problems early on.

Principles of Earned Value Management (EVM)

- **Integration:** EVM integrates cost, schedule, and scope to provide a comprehensive view of project performance.

- **Objectivity:** EVM is based on objective data, such as the planned value, actual cost, and earned value.

- **Timeliness:** EVM provides timely feedback on project performance.

- **Visibility:** EVM provides visibility into project performance for all stakeholders.

Corollaries of EVM

- **100% Rule:** The planned value (PV) must account for 100% of the project's work.

- **80/20 Rule:** 80% of the project's effort is typically spent on 20% of the work.

- **10/90 Rule:** The first 10% of the project's effort is typically spent on developing the baseline plan.

- **Scope Creep:** Scope creep is the unplanned addition of new features or requirements to a project, which can lead to delays and increased costs.

Syndromes of EVM

- **Gold Plating:** Gold plating is the tendency to exceed the requirements of a project, which can lead to delays and increased costs.

- **Perfectionism:** Perfectionism is the tendency to strive for perfection, even when it is not necessary, which can lead to delays and increased costs.

- **Analysis Paralysis:** Analysis paralysis is the tendency to spend too much time analyzing a project and not enough time taking action, which can lead to delays and increased costs.

Understanding these principles, corollaries, and syndromes can help project managers use EVM more effectively:

- **Integration:** Project managers should integrate EVM into their project management processes to ensure that cost, schedule, and scope are considered together.

- **Objectivity:** Project managers should use objective data to calculate EVM metrics, such as the planned value, actual cost, and earned value.

- **Timeliness:** Project managers should review EVM metrics regularly to identify trends and patterns early on.

- **Visibility:** Project managers should communicate EVM results to all stakeholders to keep them informed of the project's progress and to identify any potential problems early on.

Here are some additional tips for using EVM effectively:

- **Use EVM in conjunction with other project management tools and techniques.** EVM is a powerful tool, but it is not a silver bullet. Project managers should use EVM in conjunction with other project management tools and techniques, such as Gantt charts, PERT charts, and risk registers.

- **Get training on EVM.** EVM can be a complex tool, so it is important to get training on how to use it effectively.

- **Use a software tool to automate EVM calculations.** There are a number of software tools available that can automate EVM calculations. This can help to save time and reduce the risk of human error.

Scoring models

A scoring model in project management is a tool used to evaluate and rank potential projects or tasks. It is a systematic way to prioritize projects and tasks based on a set of criteria. Scoring models can be used to make decisions about which projects to fund, which tasks to complete first, and how to allocate resources.

There are many different types of scoring models, but they all work in a similar way. First, the project manager identifies the criteria that are important for the project. These criteria can include factors such as the project's cost, schedule, risk, and potential benefits.

Next, the project manager assigns a weight to each criterion. The weights indicate the relative importance of each criterion. For example, the cost criterion might be weighted more heavily than the schedule criterion if the project is on a tight budget.

Finally, the project manager assigns a score to each project or task for each criterion. The scores indicate how well the project or task meets each criterion. For example, a project with a high potential return on investment would receive a high score for the benefits criterion.

Once the scores have been assigned, the project manager calculates the total score for each project or task. The projects or tasks with the highest scores are typically given the highest priority.

Scoring models can be a very useful tool for project managers. They can help to ensure that the most important projects and tasks are completed first. Scoring models can also help to improve communication and collaboration between stakeholders.

Here is an example of a scoring model for project selection:

Criterion	Weight	Score	Total Score
Cost	30%	5	15
Schedule	20%	4	8
Risk	15%	3	4.5
Potential benefits	35%	5	17.5

Total: 45

In this example, the project with the highest total score would be given the highest priority.

Scoring models can be used to make decisions about a wide range of project management activities, including:

- Project selection
- Task prioritization
- Resource allocation
- Risk management
- Change management

Scoring models can also be used to create dashboards and reports that can be used to track project progress and identify potential problems early on.

Here are some tips for using scoring models effectively:

- Make sure that the scoring criteria are aligned with the project's goals and objectives.

- Assign weights to the criteria that reflect their relative importance.

- Use a consistent method for scoring each project or task.

- Review the scoring results regularly and make adjustments as needed.

- Communicate the scoring results to stakeholders.

Scoring models in project management can be compared and contrasted in a number of ways, including:

- **Type of model**: Scoring models can be quantitative or qualitative. Quantitative models rely on numerical data to assign scores to projects or tasks. Qualitative models rely on subjective judgments to assign scores.

- **Complexity**: Scoring models can range in complexity from simple to complex. Simple models may use a small number of criteria and assign equal weights to all criteria. Complex models may use a large number of criteria and assign different weights to each criterion.

- **Flexibility**: Scoring models can be flexible or inflexible. Flexible models can be easily adapted to different projects and situations. Inflexible models are more difficult to adapt.

Here is a table that compares and contrasts different types of scoring models in project management:

Type of model	Complexity	Flexibility
Quantitative	Low	High
Qualitative	Low	High
Weighted	Medium	Medium
Unweighted	Low	High
Simple	Low	High
Complex	Medium to high	Medium

When choosing a scoring model, it is important to consider the specific needs of the project. For example, if the project is complex and there are many different criteria to consider, it may be necessary to use a more complex model. If the project is simple and there are only a few criteria to consider, it may be possible to use a simpler model.

It is also important to consider the flexibility of the model. If the project is likely to change, it is important to choose a model that can be easily adapted. If the project is unlikely to change, it is possible to choose a less flexible model.

Here are some examples of different scoring models that can be used in project management:

- **Weighted scoring model**: This is the most common type of scoring model. In a weighted scoring model, each criterion is assigned a weight, which indicates its relative importance. The scores for each criterion are then multiplied by their respective weights and summed to calculate the total score for the project or task.

- **Unweighted scoring model**: In an unweighted scoring model, all criteria are given equal weight. The scores for each criterion are simply summed to calculate the total score for the project or task.

- **Simple scoring model**: This type of model is typically used for small and simple projects. A simple scoring model may use only a few criteria and assign equal weights to all criteria.

- **Complex scoring model**: This type of model is typically used for large and complex projects. A complex scoring model may use a large number of criteria and assign different weights to each criterion.

Guidelines for using scoring models in project management

- **Identify the criteria that are important for the project.** This may involve consulting with stakeholders to get their input.

- **Assign a weight to each criterion.** The weights should indicate the relative importance of each criterion.

- **Develop a method for scoring each project or task for each criterion.** The scoring method should be consistent and objective.

- **Calculate the total score for each project or task.** This can be done by multiplying the score for each criterion by its weight and summing the products.

- **Analyze the scoring results.** This may involve identifying the projects or tasks with the highest and lowest scores, as well as the criteria that are driving the scores.
- **Make decisions about which projects or tasks to prioritize and how to allocate resources.** The scoring results should be used to inform these decisions, but they should not be the only factor considered.

Framework for using scoring models in project management

1. **Define the project's goals and objectives.** This will help to identify the criteria that are important for the project.

2. **Identify the stakeholders.** This will help to ensure that all relevant perspectives are considered when developing the scoring model.

3. **Develop the scoring model.** This includes identifying the criteria, assigning weights, and developing a method for scoring each project or task.

4. **Score the projects or tasks.** This can be done manually or using a software tool.

5. **Analyze the scoring results.** This includes identifying the projects or tasks with the highest and lowest scores, as well as the criteria that are driving the scores.

6. **Make decisions about which projects or tasks to prioritize and how to allocate resources.** The scoring results should be used to inform these decisions, but they should not be the only factor considered.

7. **Monitor and review the scoring model.** The scoring model should be reviewed regularly to ensure that it is still relevant and effective.

Tips for using scoring models effectively

- **Involve stakeholders in the process of developing and using the scoring model.** This will help to ensure that the model is fair and that it meets the needs of all stakeholders.

- **Use objective criteria and scoring methods.** This will help to ensure that the scoring results are unbiased and reliable.

- **Regularly review and update the scoring model.** This will help to ensure that the model is still relevant and effective.

- **Use the scoring results to make informed decisions, but do not rely on them exclusively.** Other factors, such as risk and uncertainty, should also be considered when making decisions.

Principles of scoring models in project management

- **Objectivity:** Scoring models should be based on objective criteria and scoring methods. This helps to ensure that the scoring results are unbiased and reliable.

- **Transparency:** The scoring criteria and scoring methods should be transparent to all stakeholders. This helps to build trust and confidence in the scoring process.

- **Flexibility:** Scoring models should be flexible enough to be adapted to different projects and situations. This helps to ensure that the scoring model is still relevant and effective even if the project changes.

Corollaries of scoring models in project management

- **Garbage in, garbage out:** The quality of the scoring results depends on the quality of the scoring criteria and scoring methods. If the scoring criteria are not well-defined or if the scoring methods are not objective, the scoring results will be unreliable.

- **More complex does not mean better:** A more complex scoring model is not necessarily better than a simpler scoring model. A simple scoring model can be just as effective as a complex scoring model, provided that it is well-designed.

- **One size does not fit all:** There is no one-size-fits-all scoring model. The best scoring model for a particular project will depend on the specific needs of the project.

Syndromes of scoring models in project management

- **Analysis paralysis:** Project managers may become so focused on developing a perfect scoring model that they never actually start using it. This can lead to delays and increased costs.

- **Scope creep**: The scoring criteria may expand over time as new factors are added to the model. This can make the model more complex and difficult to use.

- **Gold plating**: Project managers may focus too much on the scoring results and neglect other important factors, such as risk and uncertainty. This can lead to projects that are over budget and behind schedule.

By understanding these principles, corollaries, and syndromes, project managers can use scoring models more effectively:

- Ensure that the scoring criteria and scoring methods are objective and transparent.
- Choose a scoring model that is flexible enough to be adapted to the specific needs of the project.
- Avoid analysis paralysis and scope creep by focusing on developing a simple and effective scoring model.
- Do not rely exclusively on the scoring results when making decisions. Consider other factors, such as risk and uncertainty, as well.

Cost-benefit analysis

Cost-benefit analysis (CBA) is a systematic approach to evaluating the costs and benefits of a project or investment decision. It is a valuable tool for project managers in making informed decisions about which projects to pursue and how to allocate resources.

CBA involves the following steps:

1. **Identify all of the costs and benefits associated with the project or investment.** This includes both direct and indirect costs and benefits. Direct costs are those that can be easily measured and quantified, such as material costs, labor costs, and equipment costs. Indirect costs are more difficult to measure and quantify, such as lost opportunity costs and reputational risks. Direct benefits are those that are directly related to the project or investment, such as increased revenue, reduced costs, and improved customer satisfaction. Indirect benefits are more difficult to measure and quantify, such as improved employee morale and increased innovation.

2. **Quantify the costs and benefits to the extent possible.** This may involve using a variety of methods, such as market research, financial modeling, and expert judgment.

3. **Discount the costs and benefits to present value.** This is because a dollar today is worth more than a dollar in the future due to inflation and the opportunity cost of money.

4. **Compare the discounted costs and benefits to determine the net present value (NPV) of the project or investment.** The NPV is the difference between the discounted benefits and the discounted costs. If the NPV is positive, the project or investment is expected to be profitable. If the NPV is negative, the project or investment is expected to be unprofitable.

5. **Perform a sensitivity analysis to assess the impact of uncertainty on the NPV.** This involves varying the key assumptions in the CBA to see how they affect the NPV.

6. **Make a recommendation based on the results of the CBA.** The recommendation should consider the NPV, as well as other factors such as risk, strategic alignment, and stakeholder preferences.

CBA is a powerful tool for making informed investment decisions. It can help project managers to identify the most beneficial projects, allocate resources efficiently, and mitigate risk.

Here are some examples of how CBA can be used in project management:

- **Deciding whether to launch a new product:** A company can use CBA to evaluate the costs and benefits of launching a new product, such as research and development costs, marketing costs, and expected revenue.

- **Choosing between different project alternatives**: A company can use CBA to compare the costs and benefits of different project alternatives, such as different construction methods or different software development platforms.

- **Deciding whether to invest in a new technology**: A company can use CBA to evaluate the costs and benefits of investing in a new technology, such as new manufacturing equipment or new software.

- **Making decisions about resource allocation**: A project manager can use CBA to allocate resources to the most beneficial tasks or activities.

- **Mitigating risk**: A project manager can use CBA to identify and mitigate risks by evaluating the costs and benefits of different risk mitigation strategies.

Cost-benefit analysis (CBA) can be compared and contrasted in project management in a number of ways, including:

- **Scope**: CBA can be used to evaluate a wide range of project or investment decisions, from small and simple projects to large and complex projects.

- **Complexity**: CBA can be as simple or as complex as the project or investment decision being evaluated. A simple CBA may involve only a few factors, while a complex CBA may involve many factors and sophisticated financial modeling.

- **Uncertainty**: CBA can account for uncertainty by discounting costs and benefits to present value and performing a sensitivity analysis. However, CBA cannot eliminate all uncertainty.

Here is a table that compares and contrasts CBA to other project management tools and techniques:

Tool or technique	Scope	Complexity	Uncertainty
CBA	Wide	Variable	Can account for
Gantt charts	Medium	Low	Limited
PERT charts	Medium	Medium	Limited
Risk registers	Medium	Medium	Can account for
Earned Value Management (EVM)	Medium	Medium	Can account for

CBA is a unique tool that can be used to evaluate the financial viability of a project or investment decision. It is important to note that CBA is not a silver bullet. It is important to use CBA in conjunction with other project management tools and techniques to make informed decisions.

Here are some examples of how CBA can be used to compare and contrast different project or investment decisions:

- **Deciding whether to launch two different product prototypes**: A company can use CBA to compare the costs and benefits of launching two different product prototypes. The CBA could consider factors such as the cost of developing and manufacturing each prototype, the expected sales of each product, and the profit margin on each product.

- **Choosing between two different construction methods**: A company can use CBA to compare the costs and benefits of using two different construction methods for a new building. The CBA could consider factors such as the cost of materials and labor for each method, the construction schedule for each method, and the energy efficiency of the building for each method.

- **Investing in two different software development platforms**: A company can use CBA to compare the costs and benefits of investing in two different software development platforms. The CBA could consider factors such as the cost of the software licenses, the cost of training employees, and the expected productivity gains from using each platform.

Guidelines for using cost-benefit analysis (CBA) in project management

- **Identify all of the costs and benefits associated with the project or investment.** This includes both direct and indirect costs, as well as both direct and indirect benefits.

- **Quantify the costs and benefits to the extent possible.** This may involve using a variety of methods, such as market research, financial modeling, and expert judgment.

- **Discount the costs and benefits to present value.** This is because a dollar today is worth more than a dollar in the future due to inflation and the opportunity cost of money.

- **Compare the discounted costs and benefits to determine the net present value (NPV) of the project or investment.** The NPV is the difference between the discounted benefits and the discounted costs. If the NPV is positive, the project or investment is expected to be profitable. If the NPV is negative, the project or investment is expected to be unprofitable.

- **Perform a sensitivity analysis to assess the impact of uncertainty on the NPV.** This involves varying the key assumptions in the CBA to see how they affect the NPV.

- **Make a recommendation based on the results of the CBA.** The recommendation should consider the NPV, as well as other factors such as risk, strategic alignment, and stakeholder preferences.

Framework for using CBA in project management

1. **Define the scope of the CBA.** This includes identifying the project or investment decision being evaluated and the time period over which the costs and benefits will be considered.

2. **Identify all of the costs and benefits associated with the project or investment.** This includes both direct and indirect costs, as well as both direct and indirect benefits.

3. **Quantify the costs and benefits to the extent possible.** This may involve using a variety of methods, such as market research, financial modeling, and expert judgment.

4. Discount the costs and benefits to present value.

5. Calculate the net present value (NPV) of the project or investment.

6. Perform a sensitivity analysis to assess the impact of uncertainty on the NPV.

7. Make a recommendation based on the results of the CBA.

Tips for using CBA effectively

- **Get buy-in from stakeholders.** It is important to get buy-in from stakeholders before conducting a CBA. This will help to ensure that everyone is committed to the process and that everyone understands the benefits of using CBA.

- **Use a consistent approach.** It is important to use a consistent approach to CBA across all projects and investments. This will help to ensure that the results of the CBA are comparable.

- **Document the CBA.** It is important to document the CBA process and the results of the CBA. This will help to ensure that the CBA can be audited and that the CBA can be used to make informed decisions.

Principles of cost-benefit analysis (CBA) in project management:

- **Comprehensiveness:** CBA should consider all relevant costs and benefits, both direct and indirect, tangible and intangible.

- **Objectivity:** CBA should be conducted in an objective and unbiased manner.

- **Transparency:** The assumptions and methods used in CBA should be transparent and well-documented.

- **Discounting:** CBA should discount future costs and benefits to present value, to account for the time value of money.

- **Uncertainty:** CBA should account for uncertainty by performing a sensitivity analysis.

Corollaries of CBA in project management:

- **CBA is a decision-support tool, not a decision-making tool:** CBA provides information to help decision-makers make informed decisions, but it does not make decisions on its own.

- **CBA is not a perfect tool:** CBA is a complex tool and its results are sensitive to the assumptions and methods used. Therefore, it is important to interpret the results of CBA with caution.

- **CBA should be used in conjunction with other project management tools and techniques:** CBA is a valuable tool, but it should not be used in isolation. Other project management tools and techniques, such as risk management and stakeholder engagement, should also be used to make sound project decisions.

Syndromes of CBA in project management:

- **Analysis paralysis**: Decision-makers may become so focused on the CBA process that they never actually make a decision.

- **Scope creep**: The scope of the CBA may expand over time as new factors are considered. This can make the CBA more complex and difficult to complete.

- **Gold plating**: Decision-makers may focus too much on the CBA results and neglect other important factors, such as risk and strategic alignment. This can lead to projects that are over budget and behind schedule.

By understanding these principles, corollaries, and syndromes, project managers can use CBA more effectively:

- **Ensure that the CBA is comprehensive, objective, and transparent.**

- **Use CBA to inform decision-making, but do not rely on it exclusively.**
- **Use CBA in conjunction with other project management tools and techniques.**

Payback period

The payback period in project management is the amount of time it takes for a project to generate enough cash flow to cover its initial investment. It is a simple and easy-to-calculate metric that can be used to assess the financial viability of a project and to compare different project alternatives.

To calculate the payback period, simply divide the initial investment by the annual cash flow. The payback period is expressed in years or fractions of years. For example, a project with an initial investment of $100,000 and an annual cash flow of $20,000 would have a payback period of five years.

The shorter the payback period, the more attractive the project is from a financial perspective. This is because the project will start generating a profit sooner. However, it is important to note that the payback period does not consider other important factors, such as the risk of the project and the time value of money.

Here is an example of how to use the payback period to compare two different project alternatives:

Project A	Project B
Initial investment: $100,000	Initial investment: $200,000
Annual cash flow: $20,000	Annual cash flow: $50,000
Payback period: 5 years	Payback period: 4 years

Based on the payback period alone, Project B is more attractive because it has a shorter payback period. However, it is important to consider other factors, such as the risk of each project and the time value of money, before making a final decision.

The payback period is a useful tool for project managers, but it should not be used in isolation. Other project management tools and techniques, such as net present value (NPV) and internal rate of return (IRR), should also be used to make informed project decisions.

Advantages of using the payback period:
- Simple to calculate
- Easy to understand
- Provides a quick and easy way to assess the financial viability of a project
- Can be used to compare different project alternatives

Disadvantages of using the payback period:
- Does not consider the risk of the project
- Does not consider the time value of money
- Can lead to short-term decision-making
- Can be misleading if used in isolation

The payback period in project management can be compared and contrasted in a number of ways, including:

- **Accuracy:** The payback period is a relatively simple and easy-to-calculate metric, but it is not as accurate as other project management tools, such as net present value (NPV) and internal rate of return (IRR). This is because the payback period does not consider the risk of the project or the time value of money.

- **Completeness:** The payback period only considers the cash flow of a project. It does not consider other important factors, such as the risk of the project, the strategic alignment of the project, or the impact of the project on stakeholders.

- **Suitability:** The payback period is most suitable for simple projects with short payback periods. It is not as suitable for complex projects or projects with long payback periods.

Here is a table that compares and contrasts the payback period to other project management tools and techniques:

Tool or technique	Accuracy	Completeness	Suitability
Payback period	Relatively simple and easy to calculate, but not as accurate as other methods	Only considers the cash flow of a project	Most suitable for simple projects with short payback periods
Net present value (NPV)	More accurate than the payback period, but more complex to calculate	Considers the cash flow, risk, and time value of money of a project	Suitable for a wide range of projects, including complex projects and projects with long payback periods
Internal rate of return (IRR)	More accurate than the payback period, but more complex to calculate	Considers the cash flow, risk, and time value of money of a project	Suitable for a wide range of projects, including complex projects and projects with long payback periods

When to use the payback period:

- To quickly assess the financial viability of a simple project with a short payback period.

- To compare different project alternatives with similar payback periods.

- To screen projects for further evaluation using other project management tools, such as NPV and IRR.

When not to use the payback period:

- To make final decisions about complex projects or projects with long payback periods.

- To evaluate projects with different levels of risk.

- To evaluate projects with different strategic alignments.

- To evaluate projects with different impacts on stakeholders.

Guidelines for using the payback period in project management:

- **Use the payback period in conjunction with other project management tools and techniques.** The payback period is a useful tool, but it should not be used in isolation. Other project management tools, such as net present value (NPV) and internal rate of return (IRR), should also be used to make informed project decisions.

- **Consider the risk of the project when using the payback period.** The payback period does not consider the risk of the project. Therefore, it is important to consider the risk of the project before making a decision based on the payback period.

- **Consider the strategic alignment of the project when using the payback period.** The payback period only considers the financial viability of a project. It does not consider the strategic alignment of the project. Therefore, it is important to consider the strategic alignment of the project before making a decision based on the payback period.

- **Consider the impact of the project on stakeholders when using the payback period.** The payback period only considers the financial impact of a project on the organization. It does not consider the impact of the project on other stakeholders, such as customers, employees, and the community. Therefore, it is important to consider the impact of the project on stakeholders before making a decision based on the payback period.

Framework for using the payback period in project management:

1. **Identify the project or investment decision being evaluated.**

2. **Calculate the initial investment for the project or investment decision.**

3. **Estimate the annual cash flow for the project or investment decision.**

4. **Calculate the payback period by dividing the initial investment by the annual cash flow.**

5. **Analyze the payback period.** Is it acceptable given the risk of the project, the strategic alignment of the project, and the impact of the project on stakeholders?

6. **Make a decision based on the payback period and other relevant factors.**

Tips for using the payback period effectively:

- **Use realistic estimates of the initial investment and annual cash flow.** The payback period is only as good as the estimates used to calculate it. Therefore, it is important to use realistic estimates of the initial investment and annual cash flow.

- **Consider the risk of the project when interpreting the payback period.** A shorter payback period is more attractive than a longer payback period, but this is only true if the projects have the same level of risk. If the projects have different levels of risk, it is important to consider the risk of the project when interpreting the payback period.

- **Consider the strategic alignment of the project when interpreting the payback period.** A project with a longer payback period may be more attractive if it is strategically aligned with the organization's goals and objectives. Therefore, it is important to consider the strategic alignment of the project when interpreting the payback period.

- **Consider the impact of the project on stakeholders when interpreting the payback period.** A project with a longer payback period may be more attractive if it has a positive impact on stakeholders. Therefore, it is important to consider the impact of the project on stakeholders when interpreting the payback period.

Principles of the payback period in project management:

- **Simplicity:** The payback period is a simple and easy-to-calculate metric.

- **Transparency:** The payback period is transparent and easy to understand.

- **Comparability:** The payback period can be used to compare different project alternatives.

- **Timeliness:** The payback period provides a quick and easy way to assess the financial viability of a project.

Corollaries of the payback period in project management:

- **The payback period is a measure of liquidity, not profitability.** The payback period only considers the cash flow of a project, not its profitability.

- **The payback period does not consider the risk of the project.** A project with a shorter payback period may be more risky than a project with a longer payback period.

- **The payback period does not consider the time value of money.** The payback period assumes that all cash flows are created equal, regardless of when they occur.

Syndromes of the payback period in project management:

- **Myopia:** Project managers may focus too much on the payback period and neglect other important factors, such as the risk of the project and its strategic alignment.

- **Overoptimism:** Project managers may be too optimistic when estimating the initial investment and annual cash flow for a project. This can lead to a shorter payback period than is actually achievable.

- **Manipulation:** Project managers may manipulate the payback period to make a project more attractive to decision-makers. This can be done by underestimating the initial investment or overestimating the annual cash flow.

By understanding these principles, corollaries, and syndromes, project managers can use the payback period more effectively:

- **Use the payback period in conjunction with other project management tools and techniques.** The payback period is a useful tool, but it should not be used in isolation. Other project management tools, such as net present value (NPV) and internal rate of return (IRR), should also be used to make informed project decisions.

- **Consider the risk of the project when using the payback period.** A shorter payback period is more attractive than a longer payback period, but this is only true if the projects have the same level of risk. If the projects have different levels of risk, it is important to consider the risk of the project when interpreting the payback period.

- **Consider the strategic alignment of the project when using the payback period.** A project with a longer payback period may be more attractive if it is strategically aligned with the organization's goals and objectives. Therefore, it is important to consider the strategic alignment of the project when interpreting the payback period.

- **Consider the impact of the project on stakeholders when using the payback period.** A project with a longer payback period may be more attractive if it has a positive impact on stakeholders. Therefore, it is important to consider the impact of the project on stakeholders when interpreting the payback period.

Internal Rate of Return (IRR)

Internal Rate of Return (IRR) in project management is a metric used to evaluate the profitability of a project. It is the discount rate that makes the net present value (NPV) of a project's future cash flows equal to zero. In other words, it is the rate of return that an investment is expected to generate.

IRR is a useful tool for project managers because it allows them to compare different project alternatives and to make informed decisions about which projects to pursue. It is also useful for comparing different investment opportunities.

How to calculate IRR

IRR can be calculated using a variety of methods, including:

- **Financial calculator:** Most financial calculators have a built-in IRR function.

- **Excel:** Excel has a built-in IRR function.

- **Financial modeling software:** Financial modeling software, such as Bloomberg or FactSet, can be used to calculate IRR.

To calculate IRR, simply enter the following information into the calculator or software:

- The initial investment
- The future cash flows
- The discount rate

The calculator or software will then calculate the IRR.

Interpreting IRR

A higher IRR is more attractive than a lower IRR. This is because a higher IRR indicates that the project is expected to generate a higher return on investment.

However, it is important to note that IRR is not a perfect metric. It does not consider the risk of the project or the time value of money. Therefore, it is important to use IRR in conjunction with other project management tools, such as NPV and risk analysis.

Example

The following example illustrates how to calculate and interpret IRR:

A company is considering launching a new product. The initial investment for the product is $1 million. The company expects the product to generate the following cash flows over the next five years:

Year	Cash Flow
1	$200,000
2	$300,000
3	$400,000
4	$500,000
5	$600,000

Using a financial calculator, the company calculates that the IRR for the product is 25%.

This means that the company expects the product to generate a 25% return on investment.

Advantages of using IRR

- IRR is a relatively simple and easy-to-calculate metric.

- IRR is easy to understand and interpret.

- IRR can be used to compare different project alternatives.

- IRR can be used to compare different investment opportunities.

Disadvantages of using IRR

- IRR does not consider the risk of the project.

- IRR does not consider the time value of money.

- IRR can be misleading if used in isolation.

Internal Rate of Return (IRR) in project management can be compared and contrasted to other metrics in a number of ways, including:

Accuracy: IRR is a relatively accurate metric, but it is not as accurate as other methods, such as Net Present Value (NPV). This is because IRR does not consider the risk of the project or the time value of money.

Completeness: IRR considers all of the cash flows associated with a project, but it does not consider other important factors, such as the risk of the project, the strategic alignment of the project, or the impact of the project on stakeholders.

Suitability: IRR is suitable for a wide range of projects, but it is most suitable for projects with simple cash flow patterns. It is not as suitable for projects with complex cash flow patterns or projects with long payback periods.

Here is a table that compares and contrasts IRR to other project management tools and techniques:

Tool or technique	Accuracy	Completeness	Suitability
Internal Rate of Return (IRR)	Relatively accurate, but not as accurate as NPV	Considers all of the cash flows associated with a project, but does not consider other important factors, such as risk, strategic alignment, or impact on stakeholders	Suitable for a wide range of projects, but most suitable for projects with simple cash flow patterns
Net Present Value (NPV)	More accurate than IRR	Considers all of the cash flows associated with a project, as well as risk and the time value of money	Suitable for a wide range of projects, including projects with complex cash flow patterns and projects with long payback periods
Payback period	Relatively simple and easy to calculate, but not as accurate as other methods	Only considers the cash flow of a project	Most suitable for simple projects with short payback periods

When to use IRR:

- To quickly assess the profitability of a simple project with a simple cash flow pattern.

- To compare different project alternatives with similar cash flow patterns.

- To screen projects for further evaluation using other project management tools, such as NPV.

When not to use IRR:

- To make final decisions about complex projects or projects with long payback periods.

186

- To evaluate projects with different levels of risk.

- To evaluate projects with different strategic alignments.

- To evaluate projects with different impacts on stakeholders.

Guidelines for using Internal Rate of Return (IRR) in project management:

- **Use IRR in conjunction with other project management tools and techniques.** IRR is a useful tool, but it should not be used in isolation. Other project management tools, such as Net Present Value (NPV) and risk analysis, should also be used to make informed project decisions.

- **Consider the risk of the project when using IRR. IRR does not consider the risk of the project.** Therefore, it is important to consider the risk of the project before making a decision based on IRR.

- **Consider the time value of money when using IRR.** IRR does not consider the time value of money. Therefore, it is important to use a discount rate when calculating IRR.

- **Consider the strategic alignment of the project when using IRR.** IRR only considers the financial profitability of a project. It does not consider the strategic alignment of the project. Therefore, it is important to consider the strategic alignment of the project before making a decision based on IRR.

- **Consider the impact of the project on stakeholders when using IRR.** IRR only considers the financial impact of a project on the organization. It does not consider the impact of the project on other stakeholders, such as customers, employees, and the community. Therefore, it is important to consider the impact of the project on stakeholders before making a decision based on IRR.

Framework for using Internal Rate of Return (IRR) in project management:

1. **Identify the project or investment decision being evaluated.**
2. **Gather the cash flow data for the project or investment decision.**
3. **Choose a discount rate.** The discount rate should reflect the risk of the project and the opportunity cost of the investment.
4. **Calculate the IRR using a financial calculator, Excel, or financial modeling software.**
5. **Analyze the IRR.** Is it acceptable given the risk of the project, the strategic alignment of the project, and the impact of the project on stakeholders?
6. **Make a decision based on the IRR and other relevant factors.**

Tips for using Internal Rate of Return (IRR) effectively:

- **Use realistic cash flow estimates.** The IRR is only as good as the cash flow estimates used to calculate it. Therefore, it is important to use realistic cash flow estimates.
- **Use a discount rate that accurately reflects the risk of the project and the opportunity cost of the investment.** The discount rate has a significant impact on the IRR. Therefore, it is important to use a discount rate that accurately reflects the risk of the project and the opportunity cost of the investment.

- **Consider the limitations of IRR.** IRR is a useful tool, but it has some limitations. It does not consider the risk of the project or the time value of money. Therefore, it is important to consider these limitations when using IRR.

Principles of Internal Rate of Return (IRR) in project management:

- **Profitability:** IRR is a measure of the profitability of a project or investment. It is the discount rate that makes the net present value (NPV) of a project's future cash flows equal to zero.

- **Comparability:** IRR can be used to compare different project alternatives and to make informed decisions about which projects to pursue. It is also useful for comparing different investment opportunities.

- **Flexibility:** IRR can be used to evaluate a wide range of projects and investments, including projects with complex cash flow patterns and projects with long payback periods.

Corollaries of Internal Rate of Return (IRR) in project management:

- **IRR is a measure of absolute profitability, not relative profitability.** IRR does not consider the size of the investment. Therefore, it is important to consider the size of the investment when interpreting IRR.

- **IRR does not consider the risk of the project.** A project with a higher IRR may be more risky than a project with a lower IRR.

- **IRR does not consider the time value of money.** IRR assumes that all cash flows are created equal, regardless of when they occur.

Syndromes of Internal Rate of Return (IRR) in project management:

- **IRR manipulation:** Project managers may manipulate the cash flow data or the discount rate to produce a higher IRR. This can lead to making decisions based on inaccurate information.

- **IRR myopia:** Project managers may focus too much on IRR and neglect other important factors, such as the risk of the project and its strategic alignment.

- **IRR overemphasis**: Project managers may give too much weight to IRR when making decisions. This can lead to making decisions that are not in the best interests of the organization.

By understanding these principles, corollaries, and syndromes, project managers can use Internal Rate of Return (IRR) more effectively:

- **Use IRR in conjunction with other project management tools and techniques.** IRR is a useful tool, but it should not be used in isolation. Other project management tools, such as Net Present Value (NPV) and risk analysis, should also be used to make informed project decisions.

- **Consider the risk of the project when using IRR.** A higher IRR is more attractive than a lower IRR, but this is only true if the projects have the same level of risk. If the projects have different levels of risk, it is important to consider the risk of the project when interpreting IRR.

- **Consider the strategic alignment of the project when using IRR.** A project with a lower IRR may be more attractive if it is strategically aligned with the organization's goals and objectives. Therefore, it is important to consider the strategic alignment of the project when interpreting IRR.

- **Consider the impact of the project on stakeholders when using IRR.** A project with a lower IRR may be more attractive if it has a positive impact on stakeholders. Therefore, it is important to consider the impact of the project on stakeholders when interpreting IRR.

Net present value (NPV)

Net present value (NPV) is a capital budgeting method used to evaluate the profitability of an investment or project. It discounts future cash flows to their present value using a discount rate that reflects the time value of money and the risk of the investment.

NPV is calculated using the following formula:

NPV = C (CFt / (1 + r)t)

where:

- CFt is the cash flow in year t
- r is the discount rate
- t is the number of years
  NPV is considered to be a more accurate measure of profitability

than other methods, such as payback period or internal rate of return

(IRR), because it takes into account the time value of money.

Advantages of using NPV:

- NPV is a more accurate measure of profitability than other methods because it takes into account the time value of money.
- NPV can be used to compare different project alternatives with different cash flow patterns.
- NPV is a flexible tool that can be used to evaluate a wide range of projects and investments.

Disadvantages of using NPV:

- NPV can be complex to calculate, especially for projects with complex cash flow patterns.

- NPV is sensitive to the discount rate used. A small change in the discount rate can lead to a significant change in the NPV.

When to use NPV:
- NPV is a good choice for evaluating any project or investment where the cash flow is expected to vary over time.
- NPV is particularly useful for evaluating complex projects with long payback periods.
- NPV can also be used to compare different project alternatives with different cash flow patterns.

How to use NPV in project management:

NPV can be used in project management to:

- Evaluate the profitability of a project or investment.

- Compare different project alternatives.

- Make decisions about which projects to pursue.

To use NPV in project management, the following steps should be taken:

1. Identify the cash flows associated with the project or investment.

2. Choose a discount rate. The discount rate should reflect the time value of money and the risk of the investment.

3. Calculate the NPV using a financial calculator, Excel, or financial modeling software.

4. Analyze the NPV. Is it positive or negative? A positive NPV indicates that the project or investment is expected to be

194

profitable. A negative NPV indicates that the project or investment is expected to be unprofitable.

5. Make a decision based on the NPV and other relevant factors.

Example:

A company is considering launching a new product. The initial investment for the product is $1 million. The company expects the product to generate the following cash flows over the next five years:

Year	Cash Flow
1	$200,000
2	$300,000
3	$400,000
4	$500,000
5	$600,000

Using a financial calculator, the company calculates the NPV for the product to be $1.2 million.

This means that the company expects the product to generate a net profit of $1.2 million after accounting for the initial investment and the time value of money.

Net present value (NPV) can be compared and contrasted to other project management metrics in a number of ways, including:

Metric	Accuracy	Completeness	Suitability
NPV	More accurate than other methods, such as payback period and IRR	Considers all of the cash flows associated with a project, as well as risk and the time value of money	Suitable for a wide range of projects, including projects with complex cash flow patterns and projects with long payback periods
Payback period	Relatively simple and easy to calculate, but not as accurate as NPV	Only considers the cash flow of a project	Most suitable for simple projects with short payback periods
Internal rate of return (IRR)	Relatively accurate, but not as accurate as NPV	Considers all of the cash flows associated with a project, but does not consider risk	Suitable for a wide range of projects, but most suitable for projects with simple cash flow patterns

Here is a table that compares and contrasts NPV to other project management metrics:

Metric	Advantages	Disadvantages
NPV	More accurate	Can be complex to calculate
Payback period	Simple and easy to calculate	Not as accurate
IRR	Relatively accurate	Does not consider risk

When to use NPV:

- To evaluate the profitability of a project or investment.

- To compare different project alternatives with different cash flow patterns.

- To make decisions about which projects to pursue.

When not to use NPV:

- To make quick decisions, as NPV can be complex to calculate.

- To evaluate projects with a high degree of uncertainty, as NPV is sensitive to the discount rate used.

- To evaluate projects with different levels of risk, as NPV does not consider risk.

Guidelines for using Net Present Value (NPV) in project management:

- **Use NPV in conjunction with other project management tools and techniques.** NPV is a useful tool, but it should not be used in isolation. Other project management tools, such as risk analysis and scenario planning, should also be used to make informed project decisions.

- **Consider the risk of the project when using NPV.** NPV does not consider the risk of the project. Therefore, it is important to consider the risk of the project before making a decision based on NPV.

- **Choose a realistic discount rate.** The discount rate has a significant impact on the NPV. Therefore, it is important to choose a discount rate that accurately reflects the time value of money and the risk of the project.

- **Use realistic cash flow estimates.** The NPV is only as good as the cash flow estimates used to calculate it. Therefore, it is important to use realistic cash flow estimates.

Framework for using Net Present Value (NPV) in project management:

1. **Identify the project or investment decision being evaluated.**

2. **Gather the cash flow data for the project or investment decision.**

3. **Choose a discount rate.** The discount rate should reflect the time value of money and the risk of the project.

4. **Calculate the NPV using a financial calculator, Excel, or financial modeling software.**

5. **Analyze the NPV.** Is it positive or negative? A positive NPV indicates that the project or investment is expected to be profitable. A negative NPV indicates that the project or investment is expected to be unprofitable.

6. **Make a decision based on the NPV and other relevant factors.**

Tips for using Net Present Value (NPV) effectively:

- **Use sensitivity analysis to test the impact of different discount rates and cash flow estimates on the NPV.** This will help you to understand the risks associated with the project or investment.

- **Consider the strategic alignment of the project or investment when making a decision based on NPV.** A project with a lower

NPV may be more attractive if it is strategically aligned with the organization's goals and objectives.

- **Consider the impact of the project or investment on stakeholders when making a decision based on NPV.** A project with a lower NPV may be more attractive if it has a positive impact on stakeholders.

Principles:

- **NPV is a measure of the profitability of a project or investment.** It takes into account the time value of money and the risk of the investment.

- **NPV can be used to compare different project alternatives and to make informed decisions about which projects to pursue.** It is also useful for comparing different investment opportunities.

- **NPV is a flexible tool that can be used to evaluate a wide range of projects and investments.** It can be used to evaluate projects with complex cash flow patterns and projects with long payback periods.

Corollaries:

- **NPV is a measure of absolute profitability, not relative profitability.** It does not consider the size of the investment. Therefore, it is important to consider the size of the investment when interpreting NPV.

- **NPV is sensitive to the discount rate used.** A small change in the discount rate can lead to a significant change in the NPV.

- **NPV does not consider the non-financial benefits of a project or investment.** For example, a project may have a negative NPV but may provide significant benefits to the organization, such as improving customer satisfaction or increasing brand awareness.

Syndromes:

- **NPV manipulation:** Project managers may manipulate the cash flow data or the discount rate to produce a higher NPV. This can lead to making decisions based on inaccurate information.

- **NPV myopia:** Project managers may focus too much on NPV and neglect other important factors, such as the risk of the project and its strategic alignment.

- **NPV overemphasis:** Project managers may give too much weight to NPV when making decisions. This can lead to making decisions that are not in the best interests of the organization.

Decision Tree Analysis

Decision Tree Analysis (DTA) is a tool that can be used to visually represent and analyze complex decision-making situations. It is a tree-like diagram that shows the different possible outcomes of a decision and the probabilities and costs associated with each outcome.

DTA can be used in project management to:

- Evaluate the risks and benefits of different project alternatives
- Identify the best course of action given a set of uncertainties
- Make more informed decisions about resource allocation and project scheduling

To create a DTA, project managers typically follow these steps:

1. Identify the decision that needs to be made.

2. Identify all of the possible outcomes of the decision.

3. Estimate the probabilities and costs associated with each outcome.

4. Draw a tree diagram, with the decision at the root of the tree and the possible outcomes at the leaves.

5. Calculate the expected value of each outcome by multiplying the probability of the outcome by the cost of the outcome.

6. Choose the course of action with the highest expected value.

Example:

A project manager is considering two different approaches to developing a new software product. The first approach is to develop the product in-house, and the second approach is to outsource the development to a third-party vendor.

The project manager creates a DTA to evaluate the risks and benefits of each approach. The following table shows the different possible outcomes of the decision and the probabilities and costs associated with each outcome:

Outcome	Probability	Cost
In-house development successful	70%	$1 million
In-house development unsuccessful	30%	$1.5 million
Outsourcing development successful	80%	$0.75 million
Outsourcing development unsuccessful	20%	$1.25 million

The project manager calculates the expected value of each outcome as follows:

Outcome	Expected Value
In-house development successful	($1 million x 70%) + ($1.5 million x 30%) = $1.2 million
Outsourcing development successful	($0.75 million x 80%) + ($1.25 million x 20%) = $0.8 million

Based on the DTA, the project manager should choose to outsource the development of the new software product, as it has a higher expected value.

Benefits of using DTA in project management:

- **Improved decision-making**: DTA can help project managers to make more informed decisions by providing a visual representation of complex decision-making situations and by calculating the expected value of each outcome.

- **Reduced risk**: DTA can help project managers to identify and mitigate the risks associated with different project alternatives.

- **Improved resource allocation:** DTA can help project managers to allocate resources more effectively by providing insights into the costs and benefits of different project alternatives.

- **Improved project scheduling:** DTA can help project managers to develop more realistic project schedules by taking into account the uncertainties associated with different project tasks.

Decision Tree Analysis (DTA) in project management can be compared and contrasted to other project management tools and techniques in a number of ways:

Tool or technique	Accuracy	Completeness	Suitability
DTA	Relatively accurate, but can be sensitive to the accuracy of the probability and cost estimates	Considers all of the possible outcomes of a decision, but does not consider non-financial factors	Suitable for a wide range of project management situations, but most suitable for situations where there is a high degree of uncertainty
Net Present Value (NPV)	More accurate than DTA, but more complex to calculate	Considers all of the cash flows associated with a project, as well as risk and the time value of money	Suitable for evaluating the profitability of projects, but not as suitable for evaluating projects with a high degree of uncertainty
Internal Rate of Return (IRR)	More accurate than DTA, but more complex to calculate and can be misleading	Considers all of the cash flows associated with a project, but does not consider risk	Suitable for evaluating the profitability of projects with simple cash flow patterns, but not as suitable for projects with complex cash flow patterns or projects with a high degree of uncertainty

Here is a table that compares and contrasts DTA to other project management tools and techniques:

Tool or technique	Advantages	Disadvantages
DTA	Visually represents complex decision-making situations	Can be sensitive to the accuracy of the probability and cost estimates
NPV	More accurate than DTA	More complex to calculate
IRR	More accurate than DTA	More complex to calculate and can be misleading

When to use DTA:

- To evaluate the risks and benefits of different project alternatives.

- To identify the best course of action given a set of uncertainties.
- To make more informed decisions about resource allocation and project scheduling.

When not to use DTA:

- To evaluate projects with simple cash flow patterns.

- To evaluate projects where there is a low degree of uncertainty.

Guidelines:

- **Use DTA in conjunction with other project management tools and techniques.** DTA is a useful tool, but it should not be used in isolation. Other project management tools, such as risk analysis and scenario planning, should also be used to make informed project decisions.

- **Identify all of the possible outcomes of a decision before creating a DTA.** This will help to ensure that the DTA is complete and accurate.

- **Be realistic when estimating the probabilities and costs associated with each outcome.** The accuracy of the DTA is dependent on the accuracy of these estimates.

- **Consider the non-financial factors associated with each outcome when making a decision based on a DTA.** For example, an outcome may have a negative financial impact, but it may also have positive non-financial impacts, such as improving customer satisfaction or increasing brand awareness.

Framework:

1. Identify the decision that needs to be made.

2. Identify all of the possible outcomes of the decision.

3. Estimate the probabilities and costs associated with each outcome.

4. Draw a tree diagram, with the decision at the root of the tree and the possible outcomes at the leaves.

5. Calculate the expected value of each outcome by multiplying the probability of the outcome by the cost of the outcome.

6. Choose the course of action with the highest expected value.

Tips for using DTA effectively:

- **Use sensitivity analysis to test the impact of different probability and cost estimates on the DTA.** This will help you to understand the risks associated with different project alternatives.

- **Consider using a software tool to create and analyze DTAs.** Software tools can make it easier to create and analyze complex DTAs.

- **Review the DTA with other stakeholders before making a decision.** This will help to ensure that all of the relevant perspectives have been considered.

Principles:

- **DTA is a tool for making decisions in complex and uncertain situations.**

- **DTA works by visually representing all of the possible outcomes of a decision and the probabilities and costs associated with each outcome.**

- **DTA can be used to identify the best course of action given a set of uncertainties.**

Corollaries:

- **DTA is only as good as the accuracy of the probability and cost estimates.**

- **DTA does not consider non-financial factors, such as customer satisfaction or brand awareness.**

- DTA can lead to analysis paralysis, as it can be difficult to consider all of the possible outcomes of a decision and the probabilities and costs associated with each outcome.

Syndromes:

- **DTA overload:** Project managers may try to use DTA for every decision, even when it is not necessary. This can lead to analysis paralysis and overwhelm the project team.

- **DTA misuse:** Project managers may misuse DTA by using unrealistic probability and cost estimates or by ignoring non-financial factors. This can lead to poor decision-making.

- **DTA manipulation:** Project managers may manipulate the DTA to support a predetermined decision. This can lead to unethical behavior and poor decision-making.

By understanding these principles, corollaries, and syndromes, project managers can use Decision Tree Analysis (DTA) more effectively to make informed project decisions.

Here are some tips for using DTA effectively:

- Use DTA for complex and uncertain decisions, not for every decision.

- Use realistic probability and cost estimates.

- Consider non-financial factors when making a decision.

- Review the DTA with other stakeholders before making a decision.

- Use a software tool to create and analyze complex DTAs.
- Use sensitivity analysis to test the impact of different probability and cost estimates on the DTA.

Scoring models

A scoring model in project management is a tool used to assign a numerical value to a project or task. This value can then be used to prioritize projects, evaluate different project alternatives, or make other decisions about projects.

Scoring models can be used to evaluate a wide range of factors, such as:

- **Alignment with strategic goals**
- **Financial impact**
- **Risk**
- **Technical feasibility**
- **Team resources**
- **Customer impact**

The specific factors that are included in a scoring model will depend on the needs of the organization and the specific project or task being evaluated.

There are many different types of scoring models that can be used in project management. Some of the most common types include:

- **Weighted scoring model:** This is the most common type of scoring model. It involves assigning a weight to each factor and then multiplying the weight by the factor's rating to produce a score. The scores for all factors are then added together to produce a total score for the project or task.

- **Decision matrix:** This type of scoring model is similar to a weighted scoring model, but it uses a matrix to compare different project alternatives. Each factor is assigned a column in the matrix, and each project alternative is assigned a row. The scores for each factor are then entered into the matrix. The project alternative with the highest total score is the most preferred option.

- **Pairwise comparison**: This type of scoring model involves comparing each project alternative to every other project alternative. The evaluator then assigns a score to each comparison, indicating which project alternative they prefer. The scores are then used to calculate a total score for each project alternative. The project alternative with the highest total score is the most preferred option.

How to use scoring models in project management:

To use a scoring model in project management, the following steps should be taken:

1. **Identify the factors that will be included in the scoring model.**

2. **Assign a weight to each factor.**

3. **Rate each factor for each project or task.**

4. **Calculate the score for each project or task by multiplying the weight of each factor by the factor's rating and then adding the scores for all factors.**

5. **Compare the scores for different projects or tasks to identify the best option.**

Benefits of using scoring models in project management:

There are a number of benefits to using scoring models in project management, including:

- **Improved decision-making:** Scoring models can help project managers to make more informed decisions by providing a structured way to evaluate different project alternatives.

- **Increased transparency:** Scoring models can help to increase transparency in the decision-making process by making it clear how different factors are being considered and how they are being weighted.

- **Improved communication:** Scoring models can help to improve communication between project managers and other stakeholders. By sharing the scoring model with stakeholders, project managers can help them to understand the factors that are being considered and how the decision is being made.

Scoring models in project management can be compared and contrasted in a number of ways, including:

Metric	Accuracy	Completeness	Suitability
Weighted scoring model	Relatively accurate, but can be sensitive to the accuracy of the weights and ratings	Considers all of the factors that are included in the scoring model	Suitable for a wide range of project management situations
Decision matrix	Relatively accurate, but can be complex to create and use	Considers all of the factors that are included in the scoring model	Suitable for evaluating different project alternatives
Pairwise comparison	Relatively simple to create and use, but can be less accurate than other scoring models	Does not consider all of the factors that can affect a project's success	Suitable for situations where it is necessary to quickly compare a small number of project alternatives

Here is a table that compares and contrasts different scoring models in project management:

Scoring model	Advantages	Disadvantages
Weighted scoring model	Flexible and can be adapted to different project management situations	Can be complex to create and use, and can be sensitive to the accuracy of the weights and ratings
Decision matrix	Good for comparing different project alternatives	Can be complex to create and use, and may not be suitable for situations where it is necessary to quickly evaluate a large number of project alternatives
Pairwise comparison	Simple to create and use, and can be used to quickly evaluate a large number of project alternatives	May not be as accurate as other scoring models, and does not consider all of the factors that can affect a project's success

When to use each scoring model:

- **Weighted scoring model**: When it is necessary to evaluate a wide range of factors and to produce a detailed score for each project or task.

- **Decision matrix**: When it is necessary to compare different project alternatives and to make a quick decision.

- **Pairwise comparison**: When it is necessary to quickly evaluate a large number of project alternatives and to identify the most preferred option.

Guidelines for scoring models in project management

When developing a scoring model for project management, it is important to keep the following guidelines in mind:

- **Align the model with the organization's strategic goals and objectives.** The criteria used in the model should be those that are most important to the organization in terms of achieving its goals.

- **Use objective criteria.** The criteria should be measurable and quantifiable, where possible. This will help to ensure that the scoring is consistent and fair.

- **Weight the criteria according to their importance.** Not all criteria will be of equal importance to the organization. Therefore, it is important to weight the criteria according to their relative importance.

213

- **Make the model transparent and easy to understand.** All stakeholders should be able to understand how the model works and how their input is being used.

Framework for scoring models in project management

A typical framework for scoring models in project management includes the following steps:

1. **Identify the criteria.** What are the most important factors to consider when evaluating projects? This may include factors such as strategic alignment, financial return, risk, and complexity.

2. **Define the scoring scale.** What is the range of possible scores for each criterion? For example, a scale of 1 to 5 could be used, with 5 being the highest score.

3. **Assign weights to the criteria.** This will reflect the relative importance of each criterion to the organization.

4. **Score the projects.** Evaluate each project against each criterion and assign a score.

5. **Calculate the total score for each project.** This is done by multiplying the score for each criterion by its weight and then summing the results.

6. **Rank the projects.** The projects with the highest scores are the most desirable and should be prioritized.

Example of a scoring model in project management
The following table shows an example of a scoring model for project management:

Criterion	Weight	Scoring scale
Strategic alignment	30%	1 to 5
Financial return	30%	1 to 5
Risk	20%	1 to 5
Complexity	20%	1 to 5

To use this model, each project would be evaluated against each criterion and assigned a score. For example, a project that is highly aligned with the organization's strategic goals would receive a score of 5 for strategic alignment. A project with a high potential financial return would receive a score of 5 for financial return.

Once each project has been scored, the total score is calculated by multiplying the score for each criterion by its weight and then summing the results. The projects with the highest scores are the most desirable and should be prioritized.

Principles of scoring models in project management
The following are some of the key principles of scoring models in project management:

- **Alignment with organizational goals**: The scoring model should be aligned with the organization's strategic goals and objectives. This means that the criteria used in the model should be those that are most important to the organization in terms of achieving its goals.

- **Objectivity**: The criteria used in the scoring model should be objective and measurable, where possible. This will help to ensure that the scoring is consistent and fair.

- **Transparency**: The scoring model should be transparent and easy to understand. All stakeholders should be able to understand how the model works and how their input is being used.

- **Flexibility**: The scoring model should be flexible enough to be adapted to different types of projects and different organizational contexts.

Corollaries of scoring models in project management
Some corollaries of scoring models in project management include the following:

- **Scoring models can help to improve project selection.** By using a scoring model, organizations can make more informed decisions about which projects to prioritize and invest in.

- **Scoring models can help to reduce risk.** By scoring projects against criteria such as risk and complexity, organizations can identify and mitigate potential risks early on.

- **Scoring models can help to improve communication and collaboration.** By sharing the scoring model with all stakeholders, organizations can create a common understanding of the criteria that are being used to evaluate projects. This can help to improve communication and collaboration between project managers, teams, and other stakeholders.

Syndromes of scoring models in project management
Some potential syndromes of scoring models in project management include the following:

- **Gaming the system**: Some project managers may try to "game the system" by manipulating the inputs to the scoring model in order to improve their project's score.

- **Overemphasis on certain criteria**: It is important to ensure that the scoring model does not overemphasize certain criteria, such as financial return, at the expense of other important factors, such as strategic alignment and risk.

- **Subjectivity**: Even if objective criteria are used, there may still be some element of subjectivity involved in the scoring process. It is important to be aware of this and to take steps to minimize subjectivity.

Portfolio matrix

A portfolio matrix in project management is a tool used to assess and prioritize projects based on two or more criteria. The most common portfolio matrix is the Boston Consulting Group (BCG) matrix, which uses market growth and market share to classify projects into four categories:

- **Stars**: Stars are high-growth, high-market-share projects that generate significant cash flow. These projects should be prioritized and invested in.

- **Cash cows**: Cash cows are low-growth, high-market-share projects that generate a lot of cash flow but require little investment. These projects can be used to fund other projects or to return cash to shareholders.

- **Question marks**: Question marks are high-growth, low-market-share projects. These projects require significant investment to maintain or increase their market share. Organizations should carefully consider whether to invest in question marks, as they may not be successful.

- **Dogs**: Dogs are low-growth, low-market-share projects that generate little cash flow and require significant investment. These projects should be considered for termination or divestment.

The BCG matrix is a simple but effective tool for prioritizing projects. However, it is important to note that it is not the only portfolio matrix available. Other portfolio matrices, such as the GE/McKinsey nine-cell matrix and the Arthur D. Little matrix, use different criteria to classify projects.

Here is a detailed explanation of how to use the BCG matrix in project management:

1. **Identify the criteria that you want to use to assess and prioritize your projects.** Two common criteria are strategic alignment and financial return. However, you can use any criteria that are important to your organization.

2. **Plot your projects on the BCG matrix.** To do this, assign a score to each project on each criterion. The scores should be between 1 and 5, with 5 being the highest score. Then, plot each project on the matrix, with the score for the first criterion on the x-axis and the score for the second criterion on the y-axis.

3. **Analyze the matrix and identify which projects should be prioritized.** Projects in the star quadrant should be prioritized, as they have the potential to generate significant cash flow and grow the market share of your organization. Projects in the cash cow quadrant can be used to fund other projects or to return cash to shareholders. Projects in the question mark quadrant require careful consideration, as they may require significant investment to maintain or increase their market share. Projects

in the dog quadrant should be considered for termination or divestment.

Here are some examples of how to use the BCG matrix in project management:

- A technology company might use the BCG matrix to prioritize projects that develop new products and services. The company might use strategic alignment with the company's overall strategy and the potential for financial return as the two criteria.
- A manufacturing company might use the BCG matrix to prioritize projects that improve the efficiency of its operations. The company might use cost savings and the potential for increased revenue as the two criteria.
- A healthcare organization might use the BCG matrix to prioritize projects that improve the quality of care or reduce costs. The company might use patient satisfaction and cost savings as the two criteria.

Here is a comparison and contrast of portfolio matrices in project management:

Feature	BCG Matrix	GE/McKinsey Nine-Cell Matrix	Arthur D. Little Matrix
Criteria	Market growth and market share	Industry attractiveness and business strength	Market attractiveness, competitive position, relative market share
Quadrants	Stars, cash cows, question marks, dogs	Strong growth, high market share, moderate growth, low market share, weak growth, high market share, weak growth, low market share	Emerging growth, established growth, mature growth, declining growth
Strengths	Simple and easy to understand, widely used	More detailed than the BCG matrix, considers both industry attractiveness and business strength	Considers more criteria than the BCG and GE matrices, provides a more comprehensive picture of the project portfolio
Weaknesses	Can be oversimplified, does not consider all relevant criteria	Can be complex and difficult to use, requires a lot of data	Can be time-consuming and expensive to develop and maintain

Guidelines

- **Align the portfolio matrix with the organization's strategic goals and objectives.** The criteria used in the portfolio matrix should be those that are most important to the organization in terms of achieving its goals.

- **Use objective criteria.** The criteria used in the portfolio matrix should be measurable and quantifiable, where possible. This will help to ensure that the scoring is consistent and fair.

- **Weight the criteria according to their importance.** Not all criteria will be of equal importance to the organization. Therefore, it is important to weight the criteria according to their relative importance.

- **Make the portfolio matrix transparent and easy to understand.** All stakeholders should be able to understand how the portfolio matrix works and how their input is being used.

Framework

1. **Identify the criteria that you want to use to assess and prioritize your projects.** This will depend on the specific needs of your organization.

2. **Develop a scoring scale for each criterion.** This will help you to assess each project against each criterion in a consistent and objective way.

3. **Score each project against each criterion.** This can be done by a team of experts or by a single person, depending on the size and complexity of your project portfolio.

4. **Calculate the total score for each project.** This is done by multiplying the score for each criterion by its weight and then summing the results.

5. **Plot the projects on the portfolio matrix.** This will help you to visualize the projects and identify which ones should be prioritized.

6. **Analyze the portfolio matrix and identify which projects should be prioritized.** This will depend on the specific needs of your organization. However, you may want to consider prioritizing projects that are high in both criteria, such as strategic alignment and financial return.

Once you have identified the projects that you want to prioritize, you can develop a plan to manage them effectively. This may involve allocating resources, developing timelines, and communicating with stakeholders.

Here are some additional tips for using portfolio matrices effectively:

- **Use portfolio matrices regularly.** Portfolio matrices should be used on a regular basis to ensure that the project portfolio is aligned with the organization's strategic goals and objectives.

- **Involve stakeholders.** Stakeholders should be involved in the development and use of portfolio matrices. This will help to ensure that the portfolio matrices are relevant and accurate.

- **Use portfolio matrices to make decisions.** Portfolio matrices should be used to make decisions about which projects to prioritize, invest in, or terminate.

- **Review and update portfolio matrices regularly.** Portfolio matrices should be reviewed and updated on a regular basis to ensure that they are accurate and reflect the current state of the project portfolio.

Principles of the Portfolio Matrix in Project Management

The following are some of the key principles of the portfolio matrix in project management:

- **Alignment with strategic goals:** The portfolio matrix should be aligned with the organization's strategic goals and objectives. This means that the criteria used in the matrix should be those that are most important to the organization in terms of achieving its goals.

- **Objectivity:** The criteria used in the portfolio matrix should be objective and measurable, where possible. This will help to ensure that the scoring is consistent and fair.

- **Transparency:** The portfolio matrix should be transparent and easy to understand. All stakeholders should be able to understand how the matrix works and how their input is being used.

- **Flexibility:** The portfolio matrix should be flexible enough to be adapted to different types of projects and different organizational contexts.

Corollaries of the Portfolio Matrix in Project Management

Some corollaries of the portfolio matrix in project management include the following:

- **Portfolio matrices can help to improve project selection.** By using a portfolio matrix, organizations can make more informed decisions about which projects to prioritize and invest in.

- **Portfolio matrices can help to reduce risk.** By scoring projects against criteria such as risk and complexity, organizations can identify and mitigate potential risks early on.

- **Portfolio matrices can help to improve communication and collaboration.** By sharing the portfolio matrix with all stakeholders, organizations can create a common understanding of the criteria that are being used to evaluate projects. This can help to improve communication and collaboration between project managers, teams, and other stakeholders.

Syndromes of the Portfolio Matrix in Project Management

Some potential syndromes of the portfolio matrix in project management include the following:

- **Gaming the system:** Some project managers may try to "game the system" by manipulating the inputs to the portfolio matrix in order to improve their project's score.

- **Overemphasis on certain criteria:** It is important to ensure that the portfolio matrix does not overemphasize certain

225

criteria, such as financial return, at the expense of other important factors, such as strategic alignment and risk.

- **Subjectivity**: Even if objective criteria are used, there may still be some element of subjectivity involved in the scoring process. It is important to be aware of this and to take steps to minimize subjectivity.

Project prioritization

Project prioritization is the process of identifying and ranking projects based on their importance to the organization. This involves considering a variety of factors, such as strategic alignment, financial return, risk, and complexity.

Effective project prioritization is essential for any organization that wants to achieve its goals. By prioritizing the right projects, organizations can ensure that they are investing their resources in the most important activities and that they are meeting the needs of their stakeholders.

Here is a detailed explanation of the project prioritization process:

1. **Identify the criteria that will be used to prioritize projects.** This will vary depending on the specific needs of the organization. However, some common criteria include:

   o Strategic alignment: How well does the project align with the organization's strategic goals and objectives?

   o Financial return: How much financial value is expected to be generated by the project?

   o Risk: How much risk is associated with the project?

   o Complexity: How complex is the project to implement?

2. **Weight the criteria according to their importance.** Not all criteria will be of equal importance to the organization.

Therefore, it is important to weight the criteria according to their relative importance.

3. **Score each project against each criterion.** This can be done by a team of experts or by a single person, depending on the size and complexity of the project portfolio.

4. **Calculate the total score for each project.** This is done by multiplying the score for each criterion by its weight and then summing the results.

5. **Rank the projects based on their total score.** The projects with the highest scores should be prioritized.

Once the projects have been prioritized, it is important to develop a plan to manage them effectively. This may involve allocating resources, developing timelines, and communicating with stakeholders.

Here are some additional tips for effective project prioritization:

- **Get input from stakeholders.** Stakeholders should be involved in the project prioritization process. This will help to ensure that the prioritized projects are aligned with the needs of the organization and its stakeholders.

- **Use objective criteria.** Whenever possible, objective criteria should be used to prioritize projects. This will help to ensure that the prioritization process is fair and impartial.

- **Regularly review and update priorities.** Priorities can change over time. Therefore, it is important to regularly review and update the project prioritization plan.

There are a number of different methods that can be used for project prioritization in project management. Some of the most common methods include:

- **Weighted criteria:** This method involves assigning a weight to each criterion that is important for project prioritization, such as strategic alignment, financial return, risk, and complexity. Each project is then scored against each criterion based on its importance, and the total scores are used to rank the projects.

- **Pairwise comparison:** This method involves comparing each project to every other project and assigning a score to indicate which project is more important. The scores are then used to rank the projects.

- **Analytical hierarchy process (AHP):** This method is similar to the weighted criteria method, but it uses a more complex algorithm to calculate the weights of the criteria and the scores of the projects.

- **Benefit-cost analysis:** This method involves comparing the benefits of each project to the costs of implementing it. The projects with the highest net benefits are then prioritized.

- **Risk analysis:** This method involves identifying and assessing the risks associated with each project. The projects with the highest risks are then prioritized in order to mitigate the risks early on.

The best method for project prioritization will depend on the specific needs of the organization and the projects that are being prioritized. However, all of the methods listed above can be effective if used correctly.

Here is a comparison and contrast of the four project prioritization methods described above:

Feature	Weighted criteria	Pairwise comparison	Analytical hierarchy process (AHP)	Benefit-cost analysis	Risk analysis
Complexity	Relatively simple	More complex than weighted criteria	More complex than weighted criteria and pairwise comparison	More complex than the other methods	Most complex method
Accuracy	Can be accurate if the weights and scores are assigned carefully	Can be less accurate than weighted criteria, as it relies on subjective comparisons	Can be more accurate than weighted criteria and pairwise comparison, as it uses a more complex algorithm	Can be accurate if the benefits and costs are estimated correctly	Can be accurate if the risks are identified and assessed correctly
Transparency	Can be transparent if the weights and scores are clearly documented	Can be less transparent than weighted criteria, as it can be difficult to understand how the scores are assigned	Can be more transparent than weighted criteria and pairwise comparison, as the algorithm for calculating the weights and scores is well-defined	Can be transparent if the benefits and costs are estimated in a clear and consistent manner	Can be transparent if the risks are identified and assessed in a clear and consistent manner
Suitability	Suitable for a wide range of projects	Suitable for a wide range of projects	Suitable for complex projects	Suitable for projects where the benefits and costs can be estimated	Suitable for projects where there is a high degree of risk

Guidelines for Project Prioritization in Project Management

- **Align project prioritization with the organization's strategic goals and objectives.** The projects that are prioritized should be those that will help the organization achieve its strategic goals and objectives.

- **Use objective criteria.** Whenever possible, objective criteria should be used to prioritize projects. This will help to ensure that the prioritization process is fair and impartial.

- **Consider the needs of all stakeholders.** When prioritizing projects, it is important to consider the needs of all stakeholders, including customers, employees, suppliers, and shareholders.

- **Balance short-term and long-term goals.** Project prioritization should take into account both short-term and long-term goals. Some projects may be more important in the short term, while others may be more important in the long term.

- **Be flexible.** The project prioritization process should be flexible enough to accommodate changes in the organization's environment and priorities.

Framework for Project Prioritization in Project Management

Step 1: Identify the criteria that will be used to prioritize projects. This will vary depending on the specific needs of the organization. However, some common criteria include:

- Strategic alignment: How well does the project align with the organization's strategic goals and objectives?

- Financial return: How much financial value is expected to be generated by the project?

- Risk: How much risk is associated with the project?

- Complexity: How complex is the project to implement?

- Time sensitivity: How urgent is it to complete the project?

- Customer satisfaction: How important is the project to customers?

- Employee satisfaction: How important is the project to employees?

Step 2: Weight the criteria according to their importance. Not all criteria will be of equal importance to the organization. Therefore, it is important to weight the criteria according to their relative importance.

Step 3: Score each project against each criterion. This can be done by a team of experts or by a single person, depending on the size and complexity of the project portfolio.

Step 4: Calculate the total score for each project. This is done by multiplying the score for each criterion by its weight and then summing the results.

Step 5: Rank the projects based on their total score. The projects with the highest scores should be prioritized.

Step 6: Review and update the project prioritization plan regularly. Priorities can change over time. Therefore, it is important to regularly review and update the project prioritization plan.

This framework can be used to prioritize projects of all sizes and in all industries. It is a simple but effective way to ensure that the organization is investing its resources in the most important projects.

Here are some additional tips for effective project prioritization:

- **Get input from stakeholders.** Stakeholders should be involved in the project prioritization process. This will help to ensure that the prioritized projects are aligned with the needs of the organization and its stakeholders.

- **Use data to support decisions.** Whenever possible, data should be used to support decisions about project prioritization. This will help to ensure that the decisions are objective and well-informed.

- **Communicate the project prioritization plan to stakeholders.** Once the project prioritization plan has been developed, it is important to communicate it to all stakeholders.

This will help to ensure that everyone understands the priorities and that they are working towards the same goals.

Principles of Project Prioritization in Project Management

The following are some of the key principles of project prioritization in project management:

- **Alignment with strategic goals:** The project prioritization process should be aligned with the organization's strategic goals and objectives. This means that the projects that are prioritized should be those that will help the organization achieve its goals.

- **Objectivity:** The project prioritization process should be objective and fair. This means that the criteria used to prioritize projects should be objective and that the projects should be scored against the criteria in a consistent and impartial manner.

- **Stakeholder engagement:** Stakeholders should be involved in the project prioritization process. This will help to ensure that the prioritized projects are aligned with the needs of the organization and its stakeholders.

- **Flexibility:** The project prioritization process should be flexible enough to accommodate changes in the organization's environment and priorities.

Corollaries of Project Prioritization in Project Management

Some corollaries of project prioritization in project management include the following:

- **Project prioritization can help organizations to achieve their strategic goals.** By prioritizing the projects that are most important to the organization's strategic goals, organizations can increase their chances of success.

- **Project prioritization can help organizations to make better use of their resources.** By prioritizing the most important projects, organizations can ensure that their resources are allocated to the areas where they will have the biggest impact.

- **Project prioritization can help to reduce risk.** By prioritizing projects based on their risk, organizations can identify and mitigate potential risks early on.

- **Project prioritization can help to improve communication and collaboration.** By involving stakeholders in the project prioritization process and by communicating the prioritized projects to all stakeholders, organizations can create a common understanding of the priorities and improve communication and collaboration.

Syndromes of Project Prioritization in Project Management

Some potential syndromes of project prioritization in project management include the following:

- **Short-termism:** Some organizations may focus on prioritizing short-term projects at the expense of long-term projects. This can lead to problems in the long term, as the organization may not be investing in the projects that are necessary to achieve its strategic goals.

- **Scope creep**: Some projects may experience scope creep, which is when the scope of the project increases over time. This can make it difficult to prioritize projects and to allocate resources effectively.

- **Stakeholder pressure**: Some stakeholders may pressure project managers to prioritize certain projects. This can lead to project managers prioritizing projects that are not aligned with the organization's strategic goals or that are not the most important projects to the organization.

Resource allocation

Resource allocation in project management is the process of assigning and scheduling resources such as labor, materials, and equipment to activities necessary to complete projects. It is a critical step in project planning and execution, as it ensures that the right resources are available at the right time and in the right place to support project success.

There are a number of factors that should be considered when allocating resources to projects, including:

- **Project scope**: The scope of the project will determine the types and quantities of resources that are needed.

- **Project schedule**: The project schedule will determine when the resources are needed.

- **Resource availability**: The availability of resources will determine which resources can be allocated to the project.

- **Resource costs**: The costs of resources will need to be considered when making allocation decisions.

- **Resource risks**: The risks associated with resources should be considered when making allocation decisions.

The resource allocation process typically involves the following steps:

1. **Identify the resources required for the project.** This includes identifying the types and quantities of resources, as well as the specific skills and experience required.

239

2. **Estimate the resource requirements for each project activity.** This involves estimating the amount of time, materials, and equipment that will be required for each activity.

3. **Develop a resource schedule.** This involves scheduling the resources to ensure that they are available when and where they are needed.

4. **Monitor and adjust the resource allocation plan as needed.** This is important as projects can change over time, and resource requirements may need to be adjusted accordingly.

There are a number of tools and techniques that can be used to support resource allocation in project management. These include:

- **Resource loading charts**: Resource loading charts can be used to visualize the allocation of resources to project activities over time.

- **Resource leveling**: Resource leveling is a technique used to smooth out the allocation of resources over time. This can be helpful in avoiding resource overallocation and underallocation.

- **Critical path method (CPM)**: CPM is a technique used to identify the critical tasks in a project and to schedule resources accordingly.

- **Earned value management (EVM)**: EVM is a technique used to track project progress and to identify potential resource problems.

Effective resource allocation is essential for project success. By carefully considering the factors involved and by using the appropriate tools and techniques, project managers can allocate resources effectively and efficiently.

Here are some additional tips for effective resource allocation in project management:

- **Involve stakeholders in the resource allocation process.** This will help to ensure that the resource allocation plan is aligned with the needs of the organization and its stakeholders.
- **Use a variety of data and information to support resource allocation decisions.** This will help to ensure that the decisions are objective and well-informed.
- **Be flexible and adaptable.** The resource allocation plan should be flexible enough to accommodate changes in the project's scope, schedule, and risks.
- **Communicate the resource allocation plan to all stakeholders.** This will help to ensure that everyone understands the priorities and that they are working towards the same goals.

Resource allocation in project management is the process of assigning and scheduling resources to activities necessary to complete projects. It is a critical step in project planning and execution, as it ensures that the right resources are available at the right time and in the right place to support project success.

There are a number of different approaches to resource allocation in project management. Some of the most common approaches include:

- **Top-down approach**: In this approach, resources are allocated to projects based on the organization's strategic priorities. Once the resources have been allocated to projects, project managers are responsible for developing resource schedules and managing resource utilization.

- **Bottom-up approach**: In this approach, resource requirements are estimated at the project level and then rolled up to the organizational level. This approach can be helpful in ensuring that project managers have the resources they need to complete their projects successfully.

- **Hybrid approach**: In this approach, a combination of top-down and bottom-up approaches is used. For example, the organization may allocate resources to projects based on its strategic priorities, but project managers may be given some flexibility to adjust the resource allocation plan as needed.

The best approach to resource allocation will depend on the specific needs of the organization and the projects that are being managed. However, all of the approaches listed above can be effective if used correctly.

Here is a comparison and contrast of the three resource allocation approaches:

Feature	Top-down approach	Bottom-up approach	Hybrid approach
Alignment with strategic goals	High	Medium	High
Accuracy of resource estimates	Medium	High	Medium
Flexibility	Low	High	Medium
Suitability	Suitable for organizations with a clear understanding of their strategic priorities and resource requirements	Suitable for organizations with complex projects or projects with a high degree of uncertainty	Suitable for organizations that want to balance alignment with strategic goals with flexibility

When choosing a resource allocation approach, organizations should carefully consider their specific needs and the projects that are being managed. They should also involve stakeholders in the decision-making process to ensure that the chosen approach is appropriate and supported.

In addition to the three approaches listed above, there are a number of other factors that can affect resource allocation in project management. These include:

- **Project complexity**: Complex projects require more careful resource allocation than simple projects.

- **Project uncertainty**: Projects with a high degree of uncertainty require more flexibility in resource allocation.

- **Resource availability:** Resource availability can limit the options available for resource allocation.

- **Resource costs:** The costs of resources can also limit the options available for resource allocation.

Guidelines

- **Align resource allocation with strategic goals.** Resources should be allocated to projects that support the organization's strategic goals and objectives.

- **Consider resource availability and capacity.** When allocating resources, it is important to consider the availability and capacity of resources. Resources should not be overallocated, as this can lead to delays and missed deadlines.

- **Balance resource allocation between projects.** Resources should be allocated fairly and equitably across projects. It is important to avoid over-allocating resources to one project at the expense of other projects.

- **Be flexible and adaptable.** The resource allocation plan should be flexible enough to accommodate changes in the project's scope, schedule, and risks.

- **Communicate the resource allocation plan to all stakeholders.** It is important to communicate the resource allocation plan to all stakeholders, including project managers, team members, and other stakeholders. This will help to ensure that everyone is aware of the priorities and that they are working towards the same goals.

Framework

1. **Identify the resources required for the project.** This includes identifying the types and quantities of resources, as well as the specific skills and experience required.

2. **Estimate the resource requirements for each project activity.** This involves estimating the amount of time, materials, and equipment that will be required for each activity.

3. **Develop a resource schedule.** This involves scheduling the resources to ensure that they are available when and where they are needed.

4. **Monitor and adjust the resource allocation plan as needed.** This is important as projects can change over time, and resource requirements may need to be adjusted accordingly.

Tools and techniques

There are a number of tools and techniques that can be used to support resource allocation in project management. These include:

- **Resource loading charts**: Resource loading charts can be used to visualize the allocation of resources to project activities over time.

- **Resource leveling**: Resource leveling is a technique used to smooth out the allocation of resources over time. This can be helpful in avoiding resource overallocation and underallocation.

- **Critical path method (CPM)**: CPM is a technique used to identify the critical tasks in a project and to schedule resources accordingly.

- **Earned value management (EVM)**: EVM is a technique used to track project progress and to identify potential resource problems.

Principles

- **Alignment with strategic goals**: Resource allocation should be aligned with the organization's strategic goals and objectives. This means that resources should be allocated to projects that will help the organization achieve its goals.

- **Optimality**: Resources should be allocated in a way that optimizes project performance, such as by minimizing costs, maximizing benefits, or reducing risks.

- **Flexibility:** The resource allocation plan should be flexible enough to accommodate changes in the project's scope, schedule, and risks.

- **Transparency:** The resource allocation process should be transparent and communicated to all stakeholders.

Corollaries

- **Effective resource allocation can lead to improved project performance.** By allocating resources to the right projects and activities, organizations can improve their chances of success.

- **Effective resource allocation can help to reduce risk.** By allocating resources to critical tasks and projects, organizations can reduce the risk of project failure.

- **Effective resource allocation can improve stakeholder satisfaction.** By allocating resources to projects that are important to stakeholders, organizations can improve their satisfaction with the project management process.

Syndromes

- **Resource overallocation**: Resource overallocation occurs when more resources are allocated to a project than are needed. This can lead to waste and inefficiency.

- **Resource underallocation**: Resource underallocation occurs when fewer resources are allocated to a project than are needed. This can lead to delays and missed deadlines.

- **Scope creep**: Scope creep occurs when the scope of a project increases over time. This can lead to resource overallocation and missed deadlines.

- **Gold plating**: Gold plating occurs when more resources are allocated to a project than are necessary to meet the project's requirements. This can lead to waste and inefficiency.

Risk management

Risk management in project management is the process of identifying, assessing, and responding to risks that could impact the project's success. It is an iterative process that should be conducted throughout the project lifecycle.

The five steps of the risk management process are:

1. **Identify risks.** This involves brainstorming a list of all potential risks to the project, both internal and external.

2. **Assess risks.** This involves evaluating the likelihood and impact of each risk.

3. **Prioritize risks.** This involves ranking the risks based on their likelihood and impact.

4. **Develop risk responses.** This involves developing strategies to mitigate, avoid, or transfer each risk.

5. **Monitor and control risks.** This involves tracking the risks and implementing the risk responses.

Risk management is important in project management because it can help to:

- Reduce the likelihood and impact of risks
- Improve project success rates
- Protect the project's budget and schedule
- Improve communication and collaboration among stakeholders
- Increase stakeholder confidence in the project

Some common risk management techniques include:

- **Risk avoidance:** Avoiding the risk altogether.

- **Risk mitigation:** Reducing the likelihood or impact of the risk.

- **Risk transfer:** Transferring the risk to another party.

- **Risk acceptance:** Accepting the risk and planning for its occurrence.

Project managers can use a variety of tools and techniques to support risk management, such as:

- **Risk registers:** Risk registers are used to document the identified risks, their assessments, and the planned responses.

- **Risk matrices:** Risk matrices are used to prioritize risks based on their likelihood and impact.

- **Risk response plans:** Risk response plans document the specific actions that will be taken to mitigate, avoid, or transfer each risk.

- **Risk monitoring plans:** Risk monitoring plans document how the risks will be tracked and managed throughout the project lifecycle.

Effective risk management is essential for project success. By following the risk management process and using the appropriate tools and techniques, project managers can reduce the likelihood and impact of risks and improve their chances of success.

Here are some additional tips for effective risk management in project management:

- **Involve stakeholders in the risk management process.** This will help to ensure that the identified risks are comprehensive and that the risk responses are aligned with the needs of the organization and its stakeholders.

- **Use a variety of data and information to support risk assessment and decision-making.** This will help to ensure that the risk management process is objective and well-informed.

- **Regularly review and update the risk management plan.** This is important as projects can change over time, and new risks may emerge.

- **Communicate the risk management plan to all stakeholders.** This will help to ensure that everyone is aware of the risks and the planned responses.

Risk management in project management is the process of identifying, assessing, and responding to risks that could impact the project's success. It is an iterative process that should be conducted throughout the project lifecycle.

There are a number of different approaches to risk management in project management. Some of the most common approaches include:

- **Reactive risk management:** This approach involves responding to risks after they have occurred.

- **Proactive risk management:** This approach involves identifying and mitigating risks before they occur.

- **Predictive risk management:** This approach uses data and analytics to predict the likelihood and impact of risks.

- **Adaptive risk management:** This approach involves continuously monitoring and adapting the risk management plan to changes in the project environment.

The best approach to risk management in project management will depend on the specific needs of the project and the organization. However, all of the approaches listed above can be effective if used correctly.

Here is a comparison and contrast of the four risk management approaches:

Feature	Reactive risk management	Proactive risk management	Predictive risk management	Adaptive risk management
Focus	Responding to risks after they have occurred	Identifying and mitigating risks before they occur	Predicting the likelihood and impact of risks	Continuously monitoring and adapting the risk management plan to changes in the project environment
Complexity	Less complex	More complex	More complex	More complex
Suitability	Suitable for simple projects with low risk	Suitable for complex projects with high risk	Suitable for projects with a high degree of uncertainty	Suitable for projects with a high degree of dynamism

When choosing a risk management approach, organizations should carefully consider the specific needs of the project and the organization. They should also involve stakeholders in the decision-making process to ensure that the chosen approach is appropriate and supported.

In addition to the four approaches listed above, there are a number of other factors that can affect risk management in project management. These include:

- **Project complexity**: Complex projects require more careful risk management than simple projects.

- **Project uncertainty**: Projects with a high degree of uncertainty require more flexibility in risk management.

- **Stakeholder expectations**: Organizations need to consider the expectations of stakeholders when developing and implementing a risk management plan.

- Organizational culture: The organizational culture can impact the way that risk management is approached and implemented.

Guidelines

- **Align risk management with the project's goals and objectives.** Risk management should be integrated into the project planning and execution process, and the risk management plan should be aligned with the project's goals and objectives.

- **Involve stakeholders in the risk management process.** Stakeholders can provide valuable input on the identification, assessment, and prioritization of risks.

- **Use a variety of data and information to support risk management decisions.** This could include historical data, expert judgment, and risk analysis tools.

- **Develop and implement risk response plans.** Risk response plans should be developed for each identified risk, and they should be implemented in a timely and effective manner.

- **Monitor and review the risk management plan regularly.** Risks are constantly changing, so it is important to regularly monitor and review the risk management plan to ensure that it is still effective.

Framework

The following is a framework for risk management in project management:

1. **Identify risks.** This can be done through brainstorming, risk workshops, and interviews with stakeholders.

2. **Assess risks.** This involves evaluating the likelihood and impact of each risk.

3. **Prioritize risks.** This involves ranking the risks based on their likelihood and impact.

4. **Develop risk response plans.** This involves developing strategies to mitigate, avoid, or transfer each risk.

5. **Monitor and control risks.** This involves tracking the risks and implementing the risk responses.

Tools and techniques

There are a number of tools and techniques that can be used to support risk management in project management. These include:

- **Risk registers**: Risk registers are used to document the identified risks, their assessments, and the planned responses.

- **Risk matrices**: Risk matrices are used to prioritize risks based on their likelihood and impact.

- **Risk response plans**: Risk response plans document the specific actions that will be taken to mitigate, avoid, or transfer each risk.

- **Risk monitoring plans**: Risk monitoring plans document how the risks will be tracked and managed throughout the project lifecycle.

- **Risk analysis tools**: Risk analysis tools can be used to assess the likelihood and impact of risks, as well as to develop and evaluate risk response strategies.

Principles

- **Alignment with project goals and objectives**: Risk management should be aligned with the project's goals and objectives. This means that the risks that are identified and managed should be those that could impact the project's ability to achieve its goals.

- **Holistic approach**: Risk management should be taken in a holistic manner, considering all aspects of the project, including the scope, schedule, budget, quality, and resources.

- **Proactive approach**: Risk management should be proactive, rather than reactive. This means that risks should be identified and mitigated before they occur.

- **Continuous improvement**: Risk management should be viewed as a continuous process. This means that the risk management plan should be regularly reviewed and updated to reflect changes in the project environment and the identification of new risks.

Corollaries

- **Effective risk management can lead to improved project performance.** By identifying and mitigating risks, organizations can reduce the likelihood of project failure and improve the chances of success.

- **Effective risk management can help to protect the project's budget and schedule.** By identifying and mitigating risks, organizations can avoid unexpected costs and delays.

- **Effective risk management can improve communication and collaboration among stakeholders.** By involving stakeholders in the risk management process, organizations can create a shared understanding of the risks and how they will be managed.

- **Effective risk management can increase stakeholder confidence in the project.** By demonstrating that risks are being actively managed, organizations can increase the confidence of stakeholders in the project's success.

Syndromes

- **Risk complacency:** Risk complacency occurs when organizations underestimate the likelihood or impact of risks. This can lead to a failure to take appropriate risk mitigation measures.

- **Risk aversion:** Risk aversion occurs when organizations are too focused on avoiding risks. This can lead to missed opportunities and project delays.

- **Risk overmanagement:** Risk overmanagement occurs when organizations invest too much time and resources in risk management. This can lead to project inefficiency and cost overruns.

- **Risk blindness:** Risk blindness occurs when organizations fail to identify or acknowledge risks. This can lead to project failure.

Checklists

Checklists are a simple but powerful tool that can be used in all aspects of project management. They can help project managers and team members stay organized, on track, and accountable.

Here are some of the benefits of using checklists in project management:

- **Improved organization**: Checklists can help project managers and team members keep track of all of the tasks, deadlines, and resources that need to be managed. This can help to reduce the risk of missed deadlines, forgotten tasks, and oversights.

- **Increased productivity**: Checklists can help project managers and team members to be more productive by providing a clear plan of action. This can help to reduce wasted time and effort.

- **Improved quality**: Checklists can help to improve the quality of project work by ensuring that all of the necessary steps are completed. This can help to reduce the risk of errors and omissions.

- **Increased accountability**: Checklists can help to increase accountability by providing a clear record of who is responsible for each task and when it is due to be completed. This can help to ensure that everyone is working towards the same goals and that deadlines are met.

Checklists can be used for a variety of tasks in project management, such as:

- **Project planning**: Checklists can be used to identify and document all of the tasks, deadlines, and resources that need to be managed for a project.

- **Task management**: Checklists can be used to break down large tasks into smaller, more manageable steps. This can make tasks easier to complete and track.

- **Risk management**: Checklists can be used to identify and assess risks to a project. This can help project managers to develop and implement risk mitigation strategies.

- **Quality management**: Checklists can be used to ensure that all of the necessary steps are completed to produce a high-quality product or service.

- **Communication and collaboration**: Checklists can be used to communicate tasks, deadlines, and expectations to team members and stakeholders. This can help to improve communication and collaboration.

Here are some tips for using checklists effectively in project management:

- **Be specific**: Checklists should be as specific as possible. This will help to reduce ambiguity and ensure that everyone understands what needs to be done.

- **Be realistic**: Checklists should be realistic and achievable. If a checklist is too long or unrealistic, it is less likely to be used effectively.

- **Be flexible**: Checklists should be flexible enough to be adapted to the specific needs of the project. This may involve adding or removing items from the checklist as needed.

- **Communicate the checklist to all stakeholders**: The checklist should be communicated to all stakeholders, including project team members, managers, and sponsors. This will help to ensure that everyone is aware of the tasks and deadlines.

- **Regularly review and update the checklist**: The checklist should be regularly reviewed and updated to reflect changes in the project scope, schedule, or risk profile.

Checklists are a simple but powerful tool that can be used in all aspects of project management. They can help project managers and team members stay organized, on track, and accountable.

Here is a comparison and contrast of checklists in project management:

Feature	Advantages	Disadvantages
Simplicity	Checklists are simple to create and use. They can be easily adapted to the specific needs of the project.	Checklists can be too simplistic for complex projects. They may not be able to capture all of the nuances and complexities of the project.
Versatility	Checklists can be used for a variety of tasks in project management, from planning to execution to closure.	Checklists may not be suitable for all tasks. For example, they may not be effective for tasks that require creativity or innovation.
Accountability	Checklists can help to increase accountability by providing a clear record of who is responsible for each task and when it is due to be completed.	Checklists can be ineffective if they are not used consistently. If project managers and team members do not use the checklists regularly, they may not be effective in improving project performance.

When to use checklists

Checklists are most effective when used for:

- **Repetitive tasks**: Checklists can be very effective for repetitive tasks, such as those that are performed on a regular basis. For example, a checklist could be used to ensure that all of the necessary steps are completed to start a new project or to close out a completed project.

- **Complex tasks**: Checklists can also be effective for complex tasks, but they should be used in conjunction with other project management tools and techniques. For example, a checklist could be used to break down a large task into smaller, more manageable steps.

- **Tasks with a high risk of error**: Checklists can be used to reduce the risk of errors for tasks that are critical to the project's success. For example, a checklist could be used to ensure that all of the necessary steps are completed to test a new product or service before it is released to market.

How to use checklists effectively

Here are some tips for using checklists effectively in project management:

- **Create checklists that are specific and measurable.** The checklist should clearly define the tasks that need to be completed and the criteria for determining when each task is complete.

- **Make the checklists easy to use.** The checklists should be visually appealing and easy to navigate. They should also be accessible to all project stakeholders.

- **Use checklists consistently.** The checklists should be used consistently by all project stakeholders. This will help to ensure that the project stays on track and that all of the necessary tasks are completed.

- **Update the checklists regularly.** The checklists should be updated regularly to reflect changes in the project scope, schedule, or risk profile.

Guidelines

- **Use checklists for repetitive, complex, and high-risk tasks.** Checklists are most effective for tasks that are performed on a regular basis, tasks that are complex, and tasks that are critical to the project's success.

- **Involve stakeholders in the development of checklists.** Stakeholders can provide valuable input on the tasks that need to be completed and the criteria for determining when each task is complete.

- **Make checklists specific and measurable.** Checklists should clearly define the tasks that need to be completed and the criteria for determining when each task is complete.

- **Make checklists easy to use.** Checklists should be visually appealing and easy to navigate. They should also be accessible to all project stakeholders.

- **Use checklists consistently.** Checklists should be used consistently by all project stakeholders. This will help to ensure that the project stays on track and that all of the necessary tasks are completed.

- **Update the checklists regularly.** Checklists should be updated regularly to reflect changes in the project scope, schedule, or risk profile.

Framework

1. **Identify the tasks that need to be completed.** This can be done by reviewing the project plan, breaking down complex tasks into smaller steps, and identifying tasks that are critical to the project's success.

2. **Define the criteria for determining when each task is complete.** This will help to ensure that the checklists are specific and measurable.

3. **Develop checklists for each task.** Checklists should be visually appealing and easy to navigate. They should also be accessible to all project stakeholders.

4. **Use the checklists consistently.** Checklists should be used by all project stakeholders to ensure that the project stays on track and that all of the necessary tasks are completed.

5. **Update the checklists regularly.** Checklists should be updated regularly to reflect changes in the project scope, schedule, or risk profile.

Example

Here is an example of a checklist for a project to launch a new product:

- **Task 1**: Develop a product launch plan.

- **Criteria for completion**: The product launch plan should identify the target audience, the launch date, the marketing budget, and the key performance indicators (KPIs) for the launch.

- **Task 2**: Create marketing materials.

- **Criteria for completion**: The marketing materials should be visually appealing and informative. They should also be aligned with the product launch plan.

- **Task 3**: Build the product landing page.

- **Criteria for completion**: The product landing page should be visually appealing and informative. It should also be easy to navigate and should allow users to sign up for updates about the product launch.

- **Task 4**: Launch the product.

- **Criteria for completion**: The product should be launched on time and within budget. All of the marketing materials and the product landing page should be live.

- **Task 5**: Monitor the product launch performance.

- **Criteria for completion:** The product launch performance should be monitored against the KPIs that were identified in the product launch plan.

This is just one example of a checklist that can be used in project management. Checklists can be adapted to the specific needs of any project.

Principles of Checklists in Project Management

- **Clarity:** Checklists should be clear and concise, with each task clearly defined and the criteria for completion clearly stated.

- **Completeness:** Checklists should be comprehensive, including all of the tasks that need to be completed in order to achieve the project's goals.

- **Accuracy:** Checklists should be accurate and up-to-date, reflecting the current state of the project.

- **Accessibility:** Checklists should be accessible to all project stakeholders, so that everyone is aware of the tasks that need to be completed and the criteria for completion.

- **Flexibility:** Checklists should be flexible enough to be adapted to the changing needs of the project.

Corollaries of Checklists in Project Management
- **Effective use of checklists can lead to improved project performance.** By breaking down complex tasks into smaller, more manageable steps, checklists can help to ensure

that all of the necessary tasks are completed on time and within budget.

- **Checklists can help to improve communication and collaboration among project stakeholders.** By providing a shared understanding of the tasks that need to be completed and the criteria for completion, checklists can help to reduce misunderstandings and conflicts.

- **Checklists can help to reduce the risk of errors and omissions.** By providing a step-by-step guide to completing tasks, checklists can help to ensure that all of the necessary steps are taken and that nothing is overlooked.

- **Checklists can help to increase accountability.** By providing a clear record of who is responsible for each task and when it is due to be completed, checklists can help to ensure that everyone is accountable for their work.

Syndromes of Checklists in Project Management

- **Checklist complacency:** This occurs when project managers and team members become complacent about using checklists, believing that they are no longer necessary. This can lead to errors and omissions, as well as missed deadlines.

- **Checklist overload:** This occurs when project managers and team members are overloaded with checklists, making it difficult to keep track of all of the tasks that need to be completed. This can lead to stress and burnout.

- **Checklist inflexibility:** This occurs when checklists are not updated to reflect changes in the project scope, schedule, or risk profile. This can lead to delays and missed deadlines.

- **Checklist ignorance:** This occurs when project managers and team members are not aware of the benefits of using checklists, or when they do not know how to use checklists effectively. This can lead to errors, omissions, and missed deadlines.

Analytical hierarchy process (AHP)

The Analytical Hierarchy Process (AHP) is a multi-criteria decision-making (MCDM) method that can be used in project management to prioritize projects, select alternatives, and allocate resources. It is a structured approach that allows decision-makers to break down complex decisions into smaller, more manageable components.

The AHP process consists of the following steps:

1. **Identify the decision criteria.** This involves identifying the factors that are most important to the decision.

2. **Construct a pairwise comparison matrix.** This involves comparing each criterion to every other criterion in terms of its relative importance.

3. **Determine the weights of the criteria.** This involves using the pairwise comparison matrix to calculate the relative importance of each criterion.

4. **Generate and evaluate alternatives.** This involves developing and evaluating different solutions to the decision problem.

5. **Calculate the weighted scores of the alternatives.** This involves multiplying the weight of each criterion by the rating of each alternative for that criterion.

6. **Select the best alternative.** The alternative with the highest weighted score is typically selected as the best solution.

The AHP can be used in a variety of project management applications, including:

- **Project selection:** The AHP can be used to prioritize projects based on a variety of criteria, such as strategic importance, financial return, and technical risk.

- **Alternative selection:** The AHP can be used to select the best alternative for a given project, such as the best design for a new product or the best contractor to build a new office building.

- **Resource allocation**: The AHP can be used to allocate resources to projects and tasks based on their relative importance.

The AHP is a powerful tool for making complex decisions in project management. It is a structured and transparent approach that allows decision-makers to consider all of the relevant factors and to make informed decisions.

Here is an example of how the AHP can be used in project management to select the best alternative for a new product design:

Step 1: Identify the decision criteria.

The decision criteria for selecting the best new product design might include:

- **Cost**
- **Functionality**
- **Appearance**
- **Ease of use**
- **Reliability**

Step 2: Construct a pairwise comparison matrix.

The following pairwise comparison matrix shows how each criterion is compared to every other criterion in terms of its relative importance:

Criterion	Cost	Functionality	Appearance	Ease of use	Reliability
Cost	1	2	3	4	5
Functionality	1/2	1	3	4	5
Appearance	1/3	1/3	1	2	3
Ease of use	1/4	1/4	1/2	1	2
Reliability	1/5	1/5	1/3	1/2	1

Step 3: Determine the weights of the criteria.

The weights of the criteria can be calculated using the following formula:

Weight of criterion i = (Eigenvector of criterion i) / Sum of eigenvalues of all criteria

The eigenvalues of the criteria can be calculated using a variety of methods, such as the Saaty method or the geometric mean method.

Step 4: Generate and evaluate alternatives.

The next step is to generate and evaluate different alternatives for the new product design. For example, the alternatives might be three different design concepts that have been developed by the engineering team.

Step 5: Calculate the weighted scores of the alternatives.

The weighted scores of the alternatives can be calculated using the following formula:

Weighted score of alternative j = Sum (Weight of criterion i * Rating of alternative j for criterion i)

The rating of each alternative for each criterion is typically made on a scale of 1 to 5, with 1 being the lowest rating and 5 being the highest rating.

Step 6: Select the best alternative.

The alternative with the highest weighted score is typically selected as the best solution.

The Analytic Hierarchy Process (AHP) is a multi-criteria decision-making (MCDM) method that can be used in project management to prioritize projects, select alternatives, and allocate resources. It is a structured approach that allows decision-makers to break down complex decisions into smaller, more manageable components.

Here is a comparison and contrast of AHP in project management with other approaches:

Feature	AHP
Structuredness: AHP is a highly structured approach to decision-making. This makes it relatively easy to use and understand, even for decision-makers who are not familiar with MCDM methods.	Other MCDM methods can be less structured than AHP. This can make them more difficult to use and understand, but it also gives decision-makers more flexibility in how they make their decisions.
Transparency: AHP is a very transparent approach to decision-making. All of the steps involved in the AHP process are well-defined and can be easily understood by others.	Other MCDM methods can be less transparent than AHP. This can make it difficult for others to understand how the decision was made and to verify that the decision was made fairly.
Versatility: AHP can be used in a wide variety of project management applications, including project selection, alternative selection, and resource allocation.	Other MCDM methods may be more specialized and may not be suitable for all project management applications.
Computational complexity: AHP can be computationally complex for large problems. However, there are a number of software tools available that can help to simplify the AHP process.	Other MCDM methods may be less computationally complex than AHP. However, they may also be less powerful and less versatile.

Comparison of AHP with other MCDM methods:

Method	Strengths	Weaknesses
AHP	Structured, transparent, versatile	Can be computationally complex, sensitive to subjective judgments, time-consuming
Weighted average	Simple, easy to understand	Not as versatile as AHP, can be sensitive to outliers
ELECTRE	Can handle different types of data, can be used to rank alternatives	Complex to implement, can be sensitive to parameter settings
PROMETHEE	Simple to implement, can be used to rank alternatives	Not as versatile as AHP, can be sensitive to parameter settings

Overall, AHP is a powerful and versatile MCDM method that can be used effectively in a wide variety of project management applications. However, it is important to be aware of the potential limitations of AHP, such as its computational complexity.

Here are some additional advantages and disadvantages of AHP in project management:

Advantages:

- AHP is a structured and transparent approach to decision-making.
- AHP is versatile and can be used in a wide variety of project management applications.
- AHP is well-supported by software tools.
- AHP is relatively easy to use and understand, even for decision-makers who are not familiar with MCDM methods.

Disadvantages:

- AHP can be computationally complex for large problems.
- AHP can be sensitive to the subjective judgments of the decision-makers.
- AHP can be time-consuming to implement.

Guidelines:

- **Define the decision problem clearly.** What is the decision that needs to be made? What are the different alternatives that are being considered? What are the criteria that will be used to evaluate the alternatives?

- **Structure the decision problem into a hierarchy.** The hierarchy should include the decision goal, the criteria, and the alternatives.

- **Make pairwise comparisons of the criteria.** This involves comparing each criterion to every other criterion in terms of its relative importance.

- **Assign weights to the criteria.** The weights represent the relative importance of the criteria.

- **Evaluate the alternatives against the criteria.** This involves assigning ratings to each alternative for each criterion.

- **Calculate the weighted scores of the alternatives.** This is done by multiplying the weight of each criterion by the rating of each alternative for that criterion.

- **Select the alternative with the highest weighted score.** This is the alternative that is most likely to meet the decision goal.

Explanations:

- **Pairwise comparisons:** Pairwise comparisons are made using a scale of 1 to 9, where 1 means that the first criterion is equally important to the second criterion, 3 means that the first criterion is moderately more important than the second criterion, 5 means that the first criterion is strongly more important than the second criterion, 7 means that the first criterion is very strongly more important than the second criterion, and 9 means that the first criterion is extremely more important than the second criterion.

- **Weights:** The weights are calculated using the Saaty method or the geometric mean method.

- **Ratings:** The ratings are typically made on a scale of 1 to 5, where 1 is the lowest rating and 5 is the highest rating.

- **Weighted scores:** The weighted scores are calculated by multiplying the weight of each criterion by the rating of each alternative for that criterion.

- **Selection of the best alternative:** The alternative with the highest weighted score is typically selected as the best solution.

Here are some additional tips for using AHP in project management:

- **Involve stakeholders in the AHP process.** This will help to ensure that all of the relevant perspectives are considered and that the decision is supported by all of the stakeholders.

- **Use software to support the AHP process.** This can help to simplify the calculations and to make the process more efficient.

- **Be aware of the potential limitations of AHP.** AHP can be sensitive to the subjective judgments of the decision-makers and it can be time-consuming to implement.

Principles

- **Decomposition**: AHP decomposes complex decisions into smaller, more manageable components. This makes it easier to identify and evaluate the relevant criteria and alternatives.

- **Prioritization**: AHP allows decision-makers to prioritize the criteria and alternatives based on their relative importance. This helps to ensure that the decision is focused on the most important factors.

- **Consistency**: AHP provides a mechanism for checking the consistency of the decision-maker's judgments. This helps to reduce the risk of making biased or irrational decisions.

- **Transparency**: AHP is a transparent process, meaning that all of the steps involved in the decision-making process are well-defined and can be easily understood by others. This helps to build trust and confidence in the decision.

Corollaries

- **The use of AHP can lead to improved project performance.** By making informed decisions based on a comprehensive analysis of the relevant criteria and alternatives, project managers can increase the chances of success.

- **AHP can help to reduce conflict and improve communication among stakeholders.** By involving stakeholders in the AHP process and by providing a transparent and consistent approach to decision-making, project managers can build trust and consensus among stakeholders.

- **AHP can help to improve the quality of project documentation.** By documenting the AHP process and the results of the analysis, project managers can create a valuable record of the decision-making process. This can be helpful for communicating the decision to stakeholders, for justifying the decision to management, and for learning from the decision-making process in the future.

Syndromes

- **AHP misuse:** AHP can be misused if it is not used correctly. For example, if the decision-maker's judgments are not consistent, or if the wrong criteria or alternatives are considered, then the AHP results may not be reliable.

- **AHP overload**: AHP can be complex and time-consuming to implement. This can be a problem for project managers who are already under pressure.

- **AHP overconfidence**: AHP can give project managers a false sense of confidence in their decisions. It is important to remember that AHP is a tool to support decision-making, not a replacement for good judgment.

Financial models

A financial model in project management is a tool that projects the financial performance of a project. It is used to estimate the costs, revenues, and cash flows associated with the project. Financial models can be used to make a variety of decisions, such as whether to approve a project, how to allocate resources, and how to set pricing.

Financial models in project management typically include the following components:

- **Cost estimation:** This component estimates the costs associated with the project, such as labor costs, material costs, and overhead costs.

- **Revenue estimation:** This component estimates the revenues that the project will generate.

- **Cash flow estimation:** This component estimates the cash flows associated with the project, such as when costs will be incurred and when revenues will be received.

Financial models can be used to support a variety of project management activities, including:

- **Project selection:** Financial models can be used to evaluate the profitability of different project options and to select the project that is most likely to generate the highest return on investment.

- **Resource allocation:** Financial models can be used to allocate resources to projects in a way that maximizes the overall profitability of the portfolio of projects.

- **Pricing**: Financial models can be used to set prices for products and services that are developed or delivered as part of the project.

- **Risk management**: Financial models can be used to identify and assess the risks associated with the project and to develop mitigation strategies.

- **Performance monitoring**: Financial models can be used to track the actual financial performance of the project and to identify any deviations from the plan.

Here is an example of a simple financial model for a project to develop and launch a new product:

Cost estimation:

- Labor costs: $100,000

- Material costs: $50,000

- Overhead costs: $25,000

Revenue estimation:

- Product sales: $250,000

Cash flow estimation:

- Costs incurred in year 1: $175,000

- Revenues received in year 1: $0

- Costs incurred in year 2: $0

- Revenues received in year 2: $250,000

Based on this financial model, the project is expected to be profitable, with a net profit of $75,000.

Financial models in project management are tools used to project the financial performance of a project. They estimate the costs, revenues, and cash flows associated with the project and are used to make a variety of decisions, such as whether to approve a project, how to allocate resources, and how to set pricing.

Comparison of financial models in project management:

Here is a comparison of different types of financial models in project management:

Type of model	Strengths	Weaknesses
Discounted cash flow (DCF) model	Simple to use, easy to understand, versatile	Can be sensitive to the discount rate and other assumptions
Net present value (NPV) model	Similar to the DCF model, but calculates the net present value of the project's cash flows	Can also be sensitive to the discount rate and other assumptions
Internal rate of return (IRR) model	Calculates the rate of return that the project is expected to generate	Can be complex to use and interpret
Payback period model	Calculates the time it takes for the project to generate enough cash flows to cover its initial investment	Simple to use and interpret, but does not take into account the time value of money

Contrast of financial models in project management:

The main difference between financial models in project management is the way they calculate the profitability of the project.

DCF and NPV models calculate the present value of the project's cash flows, while IRR models calculate the rate of return that the project is expected to generate. The payback period model calculates the time it takes for the project to generate enough cash flows to cover its initial investment.

Another difference between financial models is their complexity. DCF and NPV models are relatively simple to use, while IRR models can be more complex to use and interpret. The payback period model is the simplest type of financial model.

Which financial model to use:

The best financial model to use in project management depends on the specific needs of the project and the decision that is being made. For example, if the decision is whether or not to approve a project, then a DCF or NPV model is typically used. If the decision is how to allocate resources between projects, then a more complex model, such as an IRR model, may be used.

It is important to note that financial models are only as good as the assumptions that are used in the model. Therefore, it is important to carefully consider the assumptions that are being made and to use realistic estimates for the costs, revenues, and cash flows.

Guidelines:

- **Identify the purpose of the model.** What decision will the model be used to support?

- **Define the scope of the model.** What costs, revenues, and cash flows will be included in the model?

- **Gather data and make assumptions.** This will involve collecting data on the costs, revenues, and cash flows associated with the project, as well as making assumptions about the future performance of the project.

- **Build the model.** This involves developing the mathematical formulas and relationships that will be used to calculate the financial performance of the project.

- **Test the model.** This involves running the model with different inputs to ensure that it is working properly and that the results are reasonable.

- **Use the model to make decisions.** Once the model has been tested and validated, it can be used to make decisions about the project, such as whether to approve the project, how to allocate resources, and how to set pricing.

Frameworks:

There are a number of frameworks that can be used to develop and use financial models in project management. One common framework is the Project Management Institute (PMI) Financial Management Knowledge Area. This framework provides guidance on the following topics:

- **Cost estimation:** This process involves estimating the costs associated with the project, such as labor costs, material costs, and overhead costs.

- **Revenue estimation:** This process involves estimating the revenues that the project will generate.

- **Cash flow estimation:** This process involves estimating the cash flows associated with the project, such as when costs will be incurred and when revenues will be received.

- **Financial risk analysis:** This process involves identifying and assessing the risks associated with the project's financial performance.

- **Earned value management:** This process is used to track the actual financial performance of the project and to identify any deviations from the plan.

Another framework that can be used to develop and use financial models in project management is the Project Management Body of Knowledge (PMBOK) Guide. This framework provides guidance on the following topics:

- **Scope management**: This process involves defining and managing the scope of the project, including the scope of the financial model.

- **Schedule management**: This process involves developing and managing the project schedule, including the schedule for developing and using the financial model.

- **Cost management**: This process involves planning, estimating, budgeting, and controlling the costs of the project, including the costs associated with developing and using the financial model.

- **Quality management**: This process involves planning, performing, verifying, and controlling the quality of the project, including the quality of the financial model.

- **Risk management**: This process involves identifying, assessing, responding to, and monitoring the risks associated with the project, including the risks associated with the financial model.

Principles:

- **Transparency**: Financial models should be transparent and easy to understand. This means that the model should be well-documented and that the assumptions and formulas used in the model should be clearly explained.

- **Accuracy**: Financial models should be accurate and up-to-date. This means that the model should be based on the best available data and that the model should be updated regularly to reflect changes in the project.

- **Flexibility**: Financial models should be flexible enough to be adapted to changes in the project. This means that the model should be able to handle different scenarios and different assumptions.

- **Utility**: Financial models should be useful for making decisions about the project. This means that the model should provide the information that the decision-makers need in a clear and concise format.

Corollaries:

- **The use of financial models can lead to improved project performance.** By using financial models to make informed decisions about the project, project managers can increase the chances of success.

- **Financial models can help to reduce risk.** By identifying and assessing the financial risks associated with the project, project managers can develop mitigation strategies to reduce the impact of these risks.

- **Financial models can help to improve communication and collaboration among stakeholders.** By using a shared financial model, stakeholders can better understand the financial implications of the project and can work together to make informed decisions.

Syndromes:

- **Model overload**: Project managers may be tempted to use complex financial models that are more than what is needed for the project. This can lead to confusion and delays.

- **Model complacency**: Project managers may become complacent about using financial models and may not update the models regularly. This can lead to inaccurate results and poor decision-making.

- **Model misuse**: Project managers may misuse financial models by using them to justify decisions that have already been made or by using them to deceive stakeholders. This can lead to a loss of trust and credibility.